PRAISE FOR MARIA NEBRES

"I wish Maria had started this years ago. I went through a horrible divorce and lost myself. It was a long journey back to my true being. Since working with Maria she has helped me regain focus, and has brought me to many realizations about myself and authentic self. When I feel anxious or afraid I can always reach out to her and her teachings. She is so calming and helps me work through my feelings in a positive way as well as raising my awareness about why I feel the way I do. She is so approachable, calm and non-judgmental and I highly recommend her. Her knowledge, sincerity and kindness are without equal."

– Jana Allen, Entrepreneur, Real Estate

"Maria is a seasoned Human Resources Professional who demonstrates a very high level of personal integrity and determination in everything she does. Maria is thoughtful in her approach and can always be counted on to provide sound advice, guidance and good judgement in all aspects of human resource management."

– Lisa Lawrence, Human Resources Innovator and Integrator

"I had the pleasure of working with Maria at [a major financial services company]. Maria was our HR Consultant and provided exemplary service to our Operations departments and its people. Maria demonstrated an expertise in succession planning, competency-based performance analysis, motivational surveys, and performance appraisals. While working with Maria, it was evident that she contributed to the success and growth of our department and our people. Her consultation, coaching and support would benefit any organization. Over the past year and to date, I have engaged in personal coaching with her and in the short time, through her care and attention to detail, I was able to recalibrate and allow pieces of the true 'me' to come out and play again. I am noticing great things happening in the way I think and lead my life both personally and professionally."

– Wanita Fonseka, Vice President, Financial Services industry

"I have known Maria for over 13 years via our working relationship at Carea Community Health Centre. I contracted her HR services for our interim HR needs at the strategic and delivery level during a period of high growth and change, needing a seasoned professional to assess our people challenges and develop our first People Strategy as an enabler of Organizational Strategy. Maria demonstrated solid people and cultural awareness, with excellent insights into gaps, challenges, and strengths to transform the future. Later in our tenure together, Maria played an instrumental role in guiding leadership through a high change environment of the amalgamation of two organizations and cultures into one.

"Maria is a very well-respected leader by all stakeholders including staff, board, and partners. She promotes and models authentic leadership and success. Regardless of the role she fulfilled, Maria consistently demonstrates the ability to build alliances, promote effective relationships, develop others, think and act strategically for success achievement, both personally and professionally. She is engaging and strongly committed to helping people and organizations develop the bench strength to successfully meet future goals. Maria demonstrates excellent judgement, work ethic, and can effectively balance competing priorities to advance them."

– Lee Kierstead,
former Executive Director, Oshawa Community Health Centre,
former Chief Executive Officer, Carea Community Health Centre

"I have known Maria for over twenty-five years in the capacity of being her Manager, colleague and as a gained personal friend. Maria is a highly qualified Human Resources Professional with authentic skills to engage others for progress and results. Over her career, she has gained comprehensive experience in and knowledge of, but not limited to, the following HR disciplines: recruitment; employee relations; performance and change management; leadership and organization development and effectiveness; employee engagement; as well as numerous legislative policies and practices. This experience has been gained through various positions in companies ranging from Financial Services; Technology; Healthcare; etc. In each of her roles, she understood what drove success in these organizations through their people, providing Human Resources Consulting solutions in support of each of the organization's goals. Through these various positions held, as well in her own Consulting Practice, Maria has gained a reputation as a trusted advisor and innovator, with strong business acumen skills. She is keen and quick to understand the Human Resource solutions required to deal with all kinds of business situations.

"Much of Maria's success is a result of personal traits such as being introspective; adaptable; intuitive; creative; an eager learner; optimistic; trustworthy; efficient and generous as well as being an effective communicator, both written and oral with exceptional listening skills. She is confident and self-assured. She is dedicated to her own self development, as evidenced by the learning and development programs she has participated in to stay current on latest practices and trends in human resources. She is a Certified Trainer of The Success Principles, Jack Canfield Methodology; True Colors Psychometric tool for Self-Awareness as well as an accredited Interpreter and Facilitator of Facet5 Personality Assessment.

"It has been my pleasure to work with Maria over the many years I have known her and would not hesitate to highly recommend to any company looking for a well-rounded Human Resources professional to engage Maria for providing HR solutions for their business to achieve success."

– Bruce Tibbitts, retired Vice President, Human Resource,
HR Business Partner and HR Consultant

"Maria has been great to work with. She connects very well with people and they readily seek her out for advice. Maria's keen insights into human nature and her acute sense of business priorities have been extremely valuable."

– Andrew Kun, former Vice President, Research and Development,
High-tech industry (currently Registered Psychotherapist)

"Maria has a rare ability to connect with the groups that she provides service to. She can bring her extensive wealth of experience to help solve any HR and people-related issue that may be faced. She is a true people person and leverages her experience and network to solve real business problems. A delight to work with on even the most difficult task, I highly recommend Maria's work."

– Andrew Obee, President and Chief Executive Officer,
Ficanex Group of Companies

Love and the Highly Engaged Team

Love

and the

HIGHLY ENGAGED TEAM

Make a Difference
Through Your Leadership

Maria R. Nebres

NEW YORK

LONDON • NASHVILLE • MELBOURNE • VANCOUVER

Love and the Highly-Engaged Team

Make a Difference Through Your Leadership

Published in New York, New York, by Morgan James Publishing in partnership with Difference Press. Morgan James is a trademark of Morgan James, LLC. www.MorganJamesPublishing.com

ISBN 9781642796476 paperback
ISBN 9781642796483 eBook
ISBN 9781642796490 audiobook
Library of Congress Control Number: 2019943448

Cover & Interior Design by:
Christopher Kirk
www.GFSstudio.com

Morgan James is a proud partner of Habitat for Humanity Peninsula and Greater Williamsburg. Partners in building since 2006.

Get involved today! Visit
MorganJamesPublishing.com/giving-back

I dedicate this book to:

*My ultimate Source of Inspiration who made me in His own image
so that I could fully express my gratitude in the name of Love*

*My beautiful son, Joshua, who inspires me to believe -
for your brilliant beginning, your present, and future*

*My dear brothers Joel, Moses, and Darren
for your lifetime love, friendship, chivalry, protection, and generosity*

*My beloved parents Raphael and Sylvia
for your foundational love and light
that showed me the way through love and lessons*

*My Brilliant Soul-Circle
for your friendship support, love, our shared memories,
giggles, and cheers, always!*

*To all,
for your brilliant beginning, your present,
and future to make a difference*

TABLE OF CONTENTS

INTRODUCTION

"The further I wake into this life, the more I realize that God is everywhere and the extraordinary is waiting quietly beneath the skin of all that is ordinary."
— Mark Nepo, *The Book of Awakening*

Entering, Waking, Growing, Transforming

I remember as a kid, being called a "Pollyanna" (from Eleanor Porter's 1913 best-selling novel character), highly optimistic and always positive for how I saw the world. It seemed unreal to many who knew me, even annoying. I couldn't tell you why, but I was seriously hopeful for everything, despite the bumps and scrapes childhood and youth angst brought on. I maintained much of this "Pollyanna" image as I grew older, yet, for much of my early adult life, I was searching for answers on how I could be both comfortable in my own skin for a voice, to model and promote positive engagement, relationships, productivity, and success both at work and in personal life, and also help others in a meaningful way towards their own life, relationships, and success goals.

As a human resources practitioner for over 25 years across various organizations, including 15 of them in a management/leadership capacity, I've helped leaders through the employment life cycle management of hiring, promoting, relating with their people; coaching on performance management and organizational culture; implementing discipline and engagement support practices; supporting results and resilience-building through change and transitions; developing roles-based clarity, skills and work relationships; coordinating retention and executing exit strategies (terminations of employment). I've managed staff, acted as an employee relations consultant for managers and employees through employment policy-development/interpretation, codes of conduct, governance, and conflict resolutions, and collaborated with leadership structures for their workplace engagement and performance strategies. Within these technical aspects, I've also counselled, heard, and felt the personal challenges and emotional pains of both leader and employee – challenges and pains coming from home and work life intertwined, triggered in the work environment and setting off emotional-based misalignments and misunderstandings. I have witnessed their pains contributing to the depletion of true positive engagement at a level deeper than any conventional organizational system can address alone.

For years, I maintained the illusion with some leaders and colleagues that we could find the answers and be in control of sustainable workplace engagement and aligned results through sophisticated programs or systems that mapped out nicely what the organization would have in place and what people needed to do within that map. Sometimes it would work, and for most of the time – when another change was mandated such as employee cut-backs, or ways of doing things, or new business mandates for "more with less" – it didn't. Some managers/leaders would rise naturally to the occasion from their authentic self, while others would continue to struggle, often resisting a unified approach they could all agree to believing. When I finally realized that my illusion was just that – as evidenced from the continued fatigue, neutrality, and disengagement by many in these organizations – I began the most incredibly creative and productive years of my own business and personal life reflection and transition, aligned to my core purpose, love, and passion. This beginning unfolded for me, a truth: that if I was deliberate with designing my own personal life, relationships and habits, exercising patience and love, the answers would find me. And they did and continue to. It started with my committed focus on self-reflection, awareness, and acceptance of where I came from, clarifying what I truly wanted in life that stood the test of time, and learning to practice a different way of thinking, believing, and behaving from habits that served this clarity. This deliberate design, this clarity, was rooted from love.

Allow me to step back for context. Reflecting on my own childhood, I grew up in Ontario, Canada and it was no accident or entitlement according to my parents. In the early 1970's, they consciously decided that, like most immigrants, making a home in a land of opportunity would be the better way to go for raising their four children, rather than staying in my birth-land, the Philippines. I don't remember much of this move, except that I do remember Mom telling me a story in my late teens, that on that day when she came back to our native land to gather me and my two younger brothers (Dad stayed in Canada to work the two jobs he managed to acquire), the five-year-old me was carrying my youngest brother on one hip, with my middle brother to my side holding my hand for dear life, as I boldly blurted out to her in my native tongue, "Are you supposed to be our mother?" My parents had set off with my eldest brother after they were sponsored by my aunt, over a year prior. I never would have guessed I would end up looking back at this and wondering, what if we had stayed in the Philippines and how fortunate we were for an entitlement my parents really did provide for me and my brothers. What I realize today was that my parents kept a strong faith and vision for a better life, worked hard to provide for their children, did their best to keep their adult issues to themselves, and that I wouldn't be where I am today had it not been for this move, their hard work, their joyful and not so joyful ways, and their efforts to raise and guide us to continue seizing opportunities to be the best we could be for our future. In my later years, I came to learn that leadership is not too dissimilar from some fundamentals to what I realized about my parents' efforts. You must have a vision and faith. You must work hard, get things done, stay committed, keep a pulse on what requires decision, juggle a slew of tasks and routines, and keep forward. You must earn your keep in the world and the respect of others. You must be grateful for what you have. You must influence your circumstances, inspire, set boundaries, guide, develop others to be their best. You must achieve results to progress. What a list to experience! As a parent, adult, and professional in this progressive society I live in, I can truly empathize with the cathartic experience of it all.

I also realized that my parents were humans too, who had four children by their early twenties, forgot to breathe and exhale in many ways, and had some dreams that stayed dreams for the sake of maintaining what they believed was needed for a good life, out of necessity: to sacrifice such dreams for a livelihood that could sustain economic challenges for an immigrant family of six. I learned so much as the years progressed, including what I had to learn on my own as my parents grew their responsibility challenges in this new home and land, and as others' influences entered my own life. With this learning came joys, but also guilt and shame-based emotional hurts from relationships and clashes between cultural upbringing of one set of norms to another, leading my early adult years to the cross-fire, grasping for my own voice and search for meaning. I also learned that in this "land of opportunity" as I grew older and widened by a circle of pressures and influences, I had to earn my progressions and lead through my own contribution, growth, engagement, relationships, struggles, and lessons.

At least seven distinct cultures have impacted me over the years, which often collided during my identity-building (heck, I'm still building my identity)! These cultures were from norms and systems of gender, family, education, social, work, the North American "way", and the Filipino "way". For each of these cultures I was expected to play a role, each with language, a way of thinking and behaving deemed necessary for a lifestyle I could be proud of. These cultures have meshed into what has shaped much of how I view myself, others, and the world, how I strive continuously to come to a place of peace inside where I can accept my past, my present, seize my future; and most importantly, love myself.

My intention is to continue impressing upon self and others, that while I am constantly doing things toward these dreams and for big love that permeates from within, I revise from learnings. I make wholehearted attempts to share my lessons from my own stretching, struggles and points of clarity – lessons that have taught me life's brilliance when seized by conscious deliberate design. I do my best and continue to grow from each moment and its circumstances before me, to find ways to nurture relationships for the sake of making a mark I can be proud of in this world as a learner, promoter, sharer and supporter of progress for a healthy humankind. Though I have and continue to face my demons along the way in this intention, I feel proud of what I have overcome, what I can share each step of the way. I am committed to this progress path. The times I've found myself in turmoil have been plenty, and I stumble along the way, but out of these times, I am grateful for what I have learned, proud of where I end up and where I will go, because I equally recall in each moment the learnings of love and the people that have made me feel blessed. I am leading my life with high engagement and therefore achieving the relationships and outcomes I want. As cliché as it may sound, my life is like a bed of roses with its thorns, influenced by its surroundings, set in loam soil made up of sand, silt clay, organic material, water and air. It needs the right nourishment and care to keep it brilliant and safeguarded from the inevitable pesky critters and nature's circumstances that can cause it to wither and die. It takes me, as the gardener to continually ensure it's cared for just right. Sometimes it takes digging deep in the loam soil for the caring of roots. Sometimes it takes pinching away the dead petals to make room for new growth. There are times for simply appreciating the aroma and beauty as the sun embraces the rich colour of the petals. Always, it takes monitoring and regulating the nourishment and close eye on responding to the circumstantial variables and factors to sustain brilliance, with unconditional love and commitment. I have my bad days, my so-so days, my good days, and my great days. I am at the center of each of those days, with choices to make, for the sake of love. I've come to realize that it must be the same for everyone.

Over the past 25 years, as a human resources practitioner, I came to realize that beneath the roles we play and perform in our world of employment, we are all the same when it comes to genuine motivation and cravings to progress and attain positive results. Yet, I have also found that, when it comes to the juggle of work and life, many of us struggle with balancing to meet a level of engagement, progress and results that make us feel true to ourselves and our core purpose. I have realized that this struggle stems largely from inner challenges with managing personal and work-related relationships. These often collide as we fumble through it, divorcing us from our core purpose and passions, wrestling with what we really want to feel and do, versus what we end up repressing or doing just to keep up with externally-based demands, appearances and relationships. In this collision, that sense for authentic "balance" breaks down. We lose our grounding to feelings of hurt, anger, anxiety, competition, and lack of self-worth, causing us to focus on judgements and belief systems that muddle the path and do not serve our life's true purpose – towards that healthy humankind, in the context of love and joy.

From personal experience with progressing in this world, what I have come and continue to know is this: we are faced with problems to solve, roles to perform, opportunities to create. In the workplace, we must relate to people, wield influence, and produce results that is in the employment contract and within the workplace culture – and really, that is like life's contract, life's other cultures. We also have this natural interest to achieve, to make our lives better, to influence the people around us, and to contribute to the betterment of others' lives: in work, personal, relationships, community, global. Yet, not all of us are fully aware that "interest" for this better is not enough, nor is it as powerful for realizing what we want in a lasting way, as that which we can achieve from being committed to this interest for better. Some often find themselves with the dilemma of how to make things work when we have so much on our plate of wants and to-do's both personally and professionally. Add to that, for the leader, the need to influence, inspire, and motivate others to align for a greater common cause. It can seem overwhelming, causing us to grasp even tighter to this notion that we can control things and people that come into our life; that we can control time; that we can control how others think of us or do unto us. That we can summon what we truly want if we wait it out. We see this covertly and overtly in the business/career life for sure – a world seemingly unto its own for the hours of devotion we keep, the external successes (such as money, status recognition) and dramas we cling to regardless of consequences to other important aspects in our life, and the hope others can follow suit to meet our external needs. This overwhelm brings us to the point when we have lost our compass, our true purpose to connect, progress and achieve lasting success, through love and joy in all aspects of our life. If this rings true to you, read on.

***

This book is a guide on how to get started with leading a personal, inner-transformation journey. This journey is a solid basepoint to get you from where you are today to where you want to go and what you want to achieve. It can help you achieve with your team, in the quickest, most thorough, effective and lasting way possible. There are some business leaders who have already begun to live by personal transformation work, and they have gained enormous value not only for their profession and leadership role, but for their personal life as well. It is through this journey that you will discover the kind of leader in you that you were meant to be. You will learn to believe it, live by it, model it, through and through with love, connection, and joy. You will be able to help yourself and others grow authentically, with balance, clarity of purpose, and alignment to produce results you and all can be proud of. This is the journey where you will find the true source for engagement and results that makes a lasting difference.

While this book is applicable to those outside of the professional working world, it is written for you, the one who is in a leadership position who wants to turn things around for your disengaged team, starting with yourself. It is a guiding perspective with a framework for how you can make a difference as a leader through better engagement for targets that you and your team are on the hook for. It is a framework for paving way to seizing and realizing great potential in all of us.

I invite all to apply for their own journey through progress and lasting success – from current state to desired state, and all that is in between – what I call, the "gap". This gap between current and desired state is a beautiful thing, really, because it is the place in which we give ourselves the opportunity to reflect and address the core source for potential of success – the opportunity to increase capacity to reflect and see the space out of which all wisdom, great, meaningful fulfillment of great outcomes are born. It is never-ending for motivated people who want progress, least of all trying to motivate, and engage others in the process. Some, like me, may define this journey as progressing through life from a place of love and joy. Name the journey however it serves you, and I ask that you welcome my invitation to the guidance offered throughout this book. Yes, because I believe that it is from a place of love and joy where success is incubated, nurtured and unleashed. There is no time to waste and we want better, for ourselves, for others, and our environments.

The time is now to create, to lead and to influence a life full of timeless and great possibilities for balance, brilliant results, meaningful connections, engagement for all in the context of love and joy – yes, even and sometimes most especially in, the business world. Pressures for decisions and actions are inevitable in business and in life, and they come at us with every day's expectations for progress within social, marketplace, legislative, financial, and technological changes and demands. In facing these pressures, many face mental and emotional blocks that cloud clarity of reason. Many slice and dice aspects of themselves in their use of time for "life" and "work", losing their sense of self. Time is important, but what's even more critical is the quality of what we do with our time to feel whole, authentic, balanced, and connected – connected to that place inside us where love and joy begins and meets the potential for progress and authentic success. If there is anything more compelling to ignite and inspire engagement for progress, it is in the realizing the great potential of what's possible through one's whole self, one's core unique, leading talents and true purpose. This book aims to reinforce and guide from this perspective, as backed up by experts in the field of personal development and mindset transformation, and through my own experience, personally and professionally.

Yes, there is a profound relevance to a brilliant change happening now for how we deal with performing under pressure, inspiring from overcoming the challenges we face, from rising in spite of it, from breaking through to achieve results and lasting success that permeates across all areas of life's spheres, thereby fortifying a limitless source for engagement, originating from within one's self and not from external. This call for authentic, lasting success from the inside-out, through expressions of love, is at the heart of the approach outlined in this book. It is a guide for how we can help enable self and others to a limitless and sustainable engagement for results, and it's being realized now by many – a transformation movement toward a new consciousness that quiets the mind for peace, focused clarity, purpose, action, meaningful fulfillment that crosses every domain of life we choose to live and operate in. A movement that transcends current limiting thoughts and belief systems, aligned with a healthier humankind. It is a movement that urges us to learn from our past, not get stuck in it. It is a movement to make productive use of awareness and intuition with clarity of a future that ensures positive results, pulling this clarity into present moments through thoughts, beliefs, and actions that support and shape the now for the sake of realizing lasting results. This is a movement with great value for workplaces, creating better wholistic relationships and results that compel us to stick it through, for cracking the code to achieving progress, abundance in time, resources, capability, and capacity. Imagine that in the workplace. Imagine that in your personal life. Imagine having a life where you can achieve balance because you feel and are, whole. Imagine yourself without the fragmentation of who you are because you have clarity of focus and purpose in every aspect of your life, and you act from these by healthy, deliberate design, not by default. You drive brilliant results to show up because of this wholeness. Now imagine that for your team too. Imagine you and your team highly engaged from this wholeness. How great would that be?

The pages of each chapter are filled with key guiding insights to a progressive solution path, for reawakening your source of love and joy – fundamental for what I believe turbocharges the unleashing of great potential for better focus, alignment, engagement, and better results that last. This progressive solution path consequently calms the chaos borne from limiting beliefs, from lack of focus, clarity, and purpose. It inspires with a guidance that organically helps to find our way back to true meaning and fulfillment. Such guidance comes from my own experience, from others I have come across through my coaching and consulting work, and from the timeless research findings and time-tested insights of some of my favourite thought-leaders. In most cases where I reference case studies from my personal, consulting and coaching experience, names and personal information have been changed or omitted to preserve anonymity, and in some cases, several people have been condensed into one person to make a clearer, more universally personal point. There are exchanges which are recreated from memory and I have done my best to render them to the best of my human ability for the sake of the point I am intending to make.

At the end of each chapter, I illustrate ways you can apply the lessons from this guiding framework – ways to galvanize your ability to recognize the foundational pillars resident in all of us to tap into. This framework intends to illuminate and guide your solution path to resolving issues, setting and reaching end state desires, relevant use of time, energy, and how to approach engagement-dependent dilemmas that stand in the way of lasting success.

How to get the most out of this book.

This book is not a "magical quick-fix" book. Positive transformation to authentic success, sustaining engagement and results takes real ongoing inner commitment and the path is unique for each individual. From my experience and witness, there really is no such prescription; rather, it's about ongoing habits in thinking, believing, acting, from a healthy within. There are many personal transformation courses, short-term seminars out there, yet mental health issues and disengagement are still high in workplaces and in personal life. Setting aside time to discover and implement learnings, practice, continual reflection, introspection, and refinements is not personally invested in on a regular basis – and all too often, those notes taken during the seminars collect dust, somewhere in a drawer, box, or shelf. For a long while, I used to file my notes away in the garage, thinking that I'd get to it once I had the time (and I never did find the time nor the notes!). Use this book as an added guiding tool to spark you to take immediate action for yourself, on a regular and ongoing basis.

***

To help you quickly with the essentials outlined in this book, I've organized it into sections.

Section 1, Essentials for Laying the Foundation is highlighted in the first three chapters to provide a context for your call to action.

In chapter 1, we determine your call for action and why it needs to be addressed.

In chapter 2, we uncover the painful dilemmas others have faced when it comes to mobilizing success during pressured times like yours – how some continue to struggle through it and why; and how others have succeeded in turning things around with an inside-out approach.

In chapter 3, I describe an integrative and iterative framework and reveal what each phase of the framework generally focuses on for relevance to addressing your call for action.

Section II, Building the Foundation and Seizing Momentum consists of the next five chapters which address each of the important framework phase-elements you'll need to incorporate to set your path in motion while achieving positive results along the way.

In chapter 4, we apply the first phase of the framework and get started with discovering your solution path. Here, we delve into concepts that aim to help guide your mindset to zoom in on what's most important to you.

In chapter 5, we delve into plotting some key actions and measures that are needed for addressing your call for action in a lasting way.

In chapter 6, I describe and reinforce the importance of keeping committed and accountable, and how, while leveraging others' commitment and accountability which significantly improves and sustains time effectiveness, engagement and productivity for you and your team.

Chapter 7 is about the continual inner work, honouring and protecting that time in your schedule as part of your solution and ongoing leadership strategy. Here, you'll learn about energizing your goals through cultivating emotions strategically, clearing out excuses, letting go of and removing mental and emotional blocks that hold you back from resolving the source of issues and the techniques needed to address these. You'll also learn that by regularly tending to inner work, you can model what it takes to maintain a high level of aligned engagement for you and your team because of the inner work you are doing for yourself and encouraging others to do in kind for themselves.

In chapter 8, I highlight how you can recognize success clues in times of stress and why it's important to break through comfort zones, understanding that doubt and fear are matters to be faced, with fearless grit. You'll learn how to do that and model it to encourage your team to do same.

In chapter 9, I highlight the key and essential relationships to focus on and take care of. You'll also learn how to redefine the use of time by leveraging the right relationships, others' core talents, strengths, and passion, to increase high engagement so that you can focus on your core genius and role as a leader, collectively achieve aligned results and build from a sense of work-life balance, and healthy relationships.

Section III, Nurturing Success through Continuous Growth, I highlight hopeful perspectives and further guidance/support in the two remaining chapters, to ensure your brilliant journey and successes continue.

In chapter 10, I offer some straight up perspectives on the inevitable obstacles no leader is immune to when it comes to leading a team, maintaining high productivity and engagement, while taking care of your own leadership plate of deliverables. You'll also learn that you can be confident that you've got it all under control, because by applying my suggested approach, you are prepared, from the inside-out, to embrace lessons and blessings, to think and act from love, joy, and connection.

In chapter 11, I highlight that the most important resource in business is the people in it, that your own transformation and modelling is key to your leadership that makes a true difference to exponentially realizing potential for great results and engagement.

***

By the end of this book, you'll have been glad for this invitation to immerse yourself through each page that aims to guide, remind, surprise, refresh you on a leadership perspective and approach to better – better engagement, better results, better wellness for you and those you lead. This very moment is all that we have to remember what true success feels like so that we can influence our future for success.

There is a leader in all of us, and it starts with leading the first essential person from the inside-out: you. When this happens, leading others and inspiring them in a way that makes a true difference, achieves progress and lasting results, can be done so with love, joy and with a sense of connection, balance, and harmony – because this is what it takes, truly.

Section I

Essentials for Laying the Foundation

Chapter 1:

CONNECTION:
AGAINST ALL ODDS

"A great leader's courage to fulfill his vision
comes from passion, not position."
– John Maxwell *The Purposeful Leader*

We've heard the debates of whether a leader is born or made. And if you investigate it just by surfing the net, you'll easily find, as I did, the plethora of information supporting each side to the argument. While there are multiple definitions of leadership due to influences both externally and personally, the various definitions generally point that great leaders possess the ability to make strategic and visionary decisions and convince others to follow those decisions in their organization. In the workplace, leaders create a vision – sometimes involving their employees – and the given expectation is that if they can successfully get others to work toward achieving that goal, they are a great leader. When leaders can get others to work toward achieving what's been set out for the organization's sake, they do this by instilling a sense of trust, by setting direction and inspiring others to want to succeed in achieving the end-result.

Effective leaders are also capable of getting people excited and motivated to work toward a vision and goals that support it. In other words, they know how to and do influence, encourage and inspire them to complete the tasks and goals that achieve the vision. And while doing so may come more naturally to some than to others, it's never easy. Vince Lombardi, the legendary Green Bay Packers coach, once said, "Contrary to the opinion of many people, leaders are not born. Leaders are made, and they are made by effort and hard work." I add to this, my belief that when we realize that we want to be a leader, we have the potential to rise to this and we have choices to make to nurture the realization of that potential.

Views on leadership got me to thinking about the relationship between "effort and hard work" and a great leader's lasting success. How is lasting success defined within this context of leadership? There is a ton of information out there – enough to make one's head spin – which pretty much sums up that it takes the individual's efforts and hard work to make leadership successful. From the viewpoints of business leaders deemed as recognizably successful, from motivational speakers' views on what it takes to achieve success, from experts in psychology and neuroscience in their studies of human potential, mindset, emotional intelligence, and physiological correlations to performance levels – all of the information brought me to reflect on my own experiences and what I have witnessed personally. What I found is that if you look beyond the workplace, you can find that when a great leader exists in an organization, that great leader and their employees are fulfilled not only in their workplace and work, but also in their personal lives, because they love – who they are, what good they bring to the world, what they do, who they relate with. They show their love and passion, they connect with their team, they are involved in their moments, in their communities, and they express a deep clarity of true purpose, joy, and connection with others and their loved ones. When this occurs, you can see it in the person, you feel it inexplicably, and as if chalking it up that this leader "just has the knack", or "special touch". Business results don't even have to be an electrifying success, nor do the next results targets get qualified as impossible or too steep because the leader and the employee accept the outcome that they will achieve. They grow, learn from it and they move forward with passion and enthused engagement. They are also transformational, exercising self-awareness, reflection, introspection, being able to work to solve challenges by finding experiences that show that old patterns do not fit or work. They want to know what must change and maximize their team's capability and capacity, because they do this for themselves too.

True Purpose

This concept of "true purpose" is fundamental to the inner fuel of purposeful leadership. True purpose unlocks true authenticity and is fundamental to dealing effectively with demands from work and personal life. Essentially, "true purpose" is that core reason for why you do or create something, because that something is meaningful to you. True purpose is what directs and shapes your beliefs and actions to achieving brilliant results. Ask yourself what your purpose is in leadership. Ask yourself what you live for each day. A pay-raise? Retirement? Job security? Status recognition in the organization? Relationships that can get you ahead or pay the household bills? Increasing your social status? Beating yourself up with guilt and anxiety for not meeting someone else's standards or dreams? Feeling miserable because bad things happen to you and you have no control over it? If these or any externally-driven aspects are what motivate you to a thought, emotion, or response, then perhaps you've discovered the reality that they typically end in disappointment, at one point or another. Now, ask yourself what you live for each day, personally.

Anyone whose true purpose comes from a misguided sense of direction will wonder why they feel unfulfilled, or troubled, victimized, lacking what they truly want, and thereby modeling that vision out to others, to their team, and other relationships. Rather than allowing life to happen, and then leaving it up to external drivers, destiny or others to take the driver's seat, make a difference in the world by taking true leadership for your own your life and then contributing, sharing with others from that. Discover what you love and feel its importance to you – let your thoughts, beliefs and actions be guided by that. Here's another thing, you know your true purpose when you feel great in taking action towards that purpose – including stretching beyond your limits – because you value it enough to stick it through despite obstacles and challenges which are always inevitable in work and in life. With true purpose, you align your efforts, your thoughts, beliefs, behavior, and actions to serve that purpose, and it makes you feel more whole, balanced, loving, joyful, and connected.

When leaders don't stack up to this 'great leader' profile, several external factors could be at play (i.e. an organization's system, processes, beliefs, culture, relationships, family, social, global market, technology) that trigger and impact one's inner capability to handle and respond to them. But I believe this external is due to what goes into the internal – the personal, all the stuff determining the motives behind decisions and actions from within the person who was anointed as a leader. This leader, selected by another leader who (you guessed it) is also dealing with personal stuff and depending on clarity of purpose, decided to appoint that selected leader.

To the argument about whether a leader is born or made, I believe it's a bit of both because we were born with potential that can only be unleashed through conscious choices we make. To be a great leader you must want it and make efforts to continually nurture it. You must embody leadership in your personal life and in the external world.

The Right to Be All You Can Be

You may have heard someone say, "Everyone is a leader." There are varying degrees to this, and the fact remains that it is not possible to live a leader's life successfully in an organization unless you are committed to the cultivating effort involved. No person can rise to their greatest possible height in leadership talent unless they make the time for this committed effort and commit to it wholistically. Really, this is the same for anything you aspire to be in life. Wallace Wattles, a best-selling American author known for his legacy in the New Thought movement posits that, "Every person naturally wants to become all that [they are] capable of becoming; this desire to realize innate possibilities is inherent in human nature. Success in life is becoming what you want to be." With the end in mind then, if you want to be a great leader, if you want to engage your tired disengaged team for better aligned results, you need to start at the source... you. You are the person who has been appointed by the organization to bear the title of leader. It takes the right heart-centered self-knowledge to form the basis for all that is entailed toward being a great leader. At a person and heart-centered level, true success in a great leader's life is about love's complete expression of all you have and give, at your highest self through mind, emotions, soul, and body.

With the leader title that you accepted, embrace it by connecting to your true life's purpose, your passion, your love. You will find clarity and lasting results through limitless possibilities for self-engagement, for lovingly connecting with others and enabling them in their self-engagement. You will find that alignment you need around what is perfectly right for the moments in time you're faced with, for the results needed. In the context of love, you are meant to contribute in this world.

When I decided to write this book, I came across Angela Lauria and her team from her organization, The Author Incubator™, during a changing point in my life. I decided I would step into my next level of showing up in the world, personally, and professionally. In a span of two years alone, Angela has helped to create over 200 bestselling non-fiction authors who want to make a difference in the world through their message. Of the many gems of guiding support provided, one that will stay with me for as long as my motivated life exists, was when she said that my book is already written, that I needed to find my way to connecting with it. She brilliantly put it, "When you anoint yourself, you are given a new heart along with the ability to control your emotions in new ways, new words, new abilities to share your message, new followers, and new means to surround them and support them."

With this book, I invite you to enable yourself to connect with what it takes from the inside-out to express your self-anointment as a great leader, and all that it takes from within. It is your right, because it is your choice and it serves your true purpose. It serves love and it produces love's brilliant results for you and others.

Under Pressure and the Perfect Storm

> *"Rough waters are truer tests of leadership.*
> *In calm water every ship has a good captain."*
> – Swedish proverb

In October of 1991, there was this private commercial fishing vessel called the Andrea Gail whose six-man crew, after much deliberation whether to continue their journey to quickly sell their celebrated late-season catch before it got spoiled (ice machine problems faced), decided to risk sailing through an impending storm in the North Atlantic Ocean to make it back to the Gloucester, Massachusetts port. The crew underestimated the severity of the weather conditions brewing – conditions where two powerful weather fronts were converging and merging, with a hurricane to follow. A perfect storm was impending. By general definition, a perfect storm happens when several weather systems all merge or converge, creating a massive storm that can destroy everything in its swallow. After several warning attempts by surrounding ships, a series of complications followed including the breakdown of radio signals. One result was that the help-crew failed to arrive and assist, and Gail's crew was left to their heroic attempts through the monstrous waves and winds – sadly to no avail, leading to the tragic demise of no survivors.

When the analogy of a "perfect storm" is applied to a leader's life, what pressures converge or merge that create disaster rather than ideal results for you, for the team, for the organization? For instance, an economic recession, political upheaval, missed financial targets, or relationship breakdowns are external pressures and can converge with the individual's inner, personal dimensions of leadership capacity and capability – causing unfavourable and disastrous results. This perfect storm can result from convergence of external pressures with the inner chaos inherent within a leader, as a person – your emotions, motives, thoughts, behaviour, habits, personal style. When all of these things converge a perfect storm could have the potential to brew, or maybe it already is brewing.

Internal and External Forces at Play

In my years of experiencing, witnessing and studying authentic success, I've learned that leaders face a multitude of conflicting pressures in their role as a leader, pressures coming from each of their leadership accountabilities for the organization such as administration, governance, mandates from divisional or departmental leadership accountability, as well as from their personal life such as caregiving, personal relationships, unresolved past experiences and household financial obligations to name a few. These pressures impose on inner capabilities and capacity to effectively handle issues and circumstances requiring effective decision-making and action-taking. The demands can be overwhelming and can cause on to lose sight of their own internal compass (true purpose, passion, love, and joy).

For many, these demands bring about layers of work and personal dilemmas that they struggle to manage, forcing decisions and actions that may undermine the leader's purpose for the organization, for their personal life of meaning. When inner leadership is not steady or balanced, one's true purpose is not part of decision-making processes; rather it's disregarded, or an after-thought. This, in turn, creates the ripple effects of unfavourable actions made across the organization, at home and with personal relationships.

When the internal turmoil is not resolved, it causes decisions and actions that get in the way of a level of leadership needed for consistent balance, engagement and sustainable results. A leader's capacity is reached and the capability for sustainable, effective leadership is compromised. I have come across some of these leaders who hold on to the position of "Why bother, that sounds like too much work and we have more important things to focus on, our customers, our shareholders/funders." Some leaders are skeptical and think, "Is this really achievable when I myself have so much on my plate, let alone seeing how tired and disengaged my teams already are?" Others may claim, "These folks simply need to be replaced if they're not producing." Some others reserve input for fear their view may be contrary to influential others' or their direct leader's view. There are also some who may not think much about it, and if they do, it's a passing thought, believing that there's a model out there that they can quickly cloak themselves with, at convenient times. Some may even think that someone else is responsible for it, otherwise it'll get fixed on its own. And then there are those who hold on to what once worked despite its expired relevance for the organization and its people in present day. They feel nostalgically comfortable with the ways things were always done, simply because that's what they know and "If it ain't broke, don't' fix it". Last but not least, I've come across some who review and pay more attention to engagement results coming from the larger mass level (their employee-base), with minimal regard for their own score-results and how these results effect their team. Here, I would posit that if you care about your team's engagement level, it's imperative to, first and foremost, care about your own, that of your fellow colleagues' in leadership positions, and that of your senior executives. Then compare those levels with your team's – review the variance, discrepancy, integrate all scores for the whole picture, and consider an integrative approach for improvements.

***

Ask yourself, what is your personal engagement level like? Are there any personal pressure points that limit you from making the right choices in the workplace, at home, in your personal life? Where are these personal pressure points coming from? What is your personal/ home life like and are there unresolved matters here that are distracting you? Do you know if you are transferring unresolved negative feelings between work and personal life? Where are these negative feelings sourced from? How well do you know yourself at core, in terms of what truly makes you happy, your true passions and purpose, and how that stacks up in what and where you are today? How far removed do you feel from your true passions and purpose? If you were to rate your own engagement level, before starting the clock on your organizational leadership role/job, what would your engagement in life and relationships be like on a scale from one to ten – one being low and ten being exceptional. These are some of the important questions to personally explore and become aware of, to seek guidance on for keeping top of mind and addressing regularly, because they get to the heart of what you can control for and engagement and success. The heart of what you can control lies in your thoughts, behaviour, emotions, belief systems, and mental images for your vision of what you want and how you will commit to achieve it.

I've witnessed the handling of dilemmas leading some organizations to worrisome outcomes with their human resources (their workforce, their people) such as unnecessary and high turnover, low productivity and engagement levels from those direct reports who were once hopeful and viewed as talented; covert and overt in-fighting; lack of communication between and among groups and teams; missed targets; increased severance costs; an unnecessary unionized environment; and a workplace on the verge, or at the point of toxic relationships fostering more disengagement and luck of trust. These are all far from the vision wanted. These are all far form an environment that fosters love and joy. Discovering and addressing why this occurs and how to mitigate requires measures that include personal engagement, mindset transformation for aligned engagement and results.

Missing Links

What we still find in today's business world is the discrepancy that exists between what many managers and leaders focus on and what their teams focus on, actually want and need, to sustain high engagement and productivity. Larger organizations and those with multiple locations certainly have a tall order in this arena also – the sense of belonging and aligned engagement can get lost even more so. Key reasons for this discrepancy are usually chalked up to limited or lack of leadership demonstration of commitment for being a part of and fostering heartful communication, leader-employee relationship nurturance, and/or provision of required meaningful support resources such as work equipment, tools, clear directives, and commitment to values. While these are true, they are not the source of the issue. The source of the issue lies in a mindset that fosters fear and disconnect, arising from issues around mis-directed attachment, identification, feelings of being threatened by situations and others, whether in the workplace or in personal life spaces. Recent Gallup research (October 2018) reports that 70% of the variance in employee engagement is due to the manager and their relationship with their staff. What it does not account for is a potential variance in personal engagement within each individual to begin with.

Many times, it is a missed opportunity to consider workplace engagement results along with where staff and leaders' personal engagement levels are in relation to these scores. Consider personal engagement to ongoing support of personal aspects such as the individual's mental health and well-being. For instance, a client of mine from an investment firm recalls the routine she experiences with her senior colleagues. In their leadership strategy meetings, they review employee engagement scores or "temperature check" results of where their employees stand with morale and productivity, yet little time is spent in meaningful discussions for how and why their leadership could be contributing to these results, their people and cultural practices for collectively supporting success from within each individual, including themselves. What she has also found particularly interesting is that when reviewed, management level scores are high, yet their mass employees' show scores that have a high variance in relation to overall leadership/management results. In other words, the mass employee scores were far lower. What's more, while leadership off-site retreats take place for development and planning, much of the focus is on reviewing business results for client scores and how processes and teams can improve their productivity for present and future targets. She recalls how personal reflection and development are rarely discussed at a deep level for ongoing and integrative transformation support strategies to link outcomes and measures in engagement results scores.

When there is a discrepancy in engagement focus between manager and employee it's important to focus on why this exists and how at the person-level it may need to be addressed on a transformative, more regular basis. The variance in engagement levels across tells an organization-wide story, a local-specific story, and a personal story each warranting deeper review for solutions. Within these variances and stories lie the personal and heart-centred level issues that are getting in the way for the great leader profile and the highly-engaged team. Everyone's individual part and responsibility cannot be addressed by anyone else but that respective individual, yet it can be supported by the organization, starting with leadership. Some leaders feel that their time is too crunched for more to do, imposing on their reserved time for something more important that cannot be collaborated on, delegated, or dismissed. This models the behavior and belief that does not allow for self and others to operate from their core genius (the core talents and skills inherent), passion, and purpose. It models the belief that no one is responsible for the underlying personal components when it comes to engagement issues or preparing – from within – for true, lasting success. If you want to own the benefits of a highly-engaged team, you also need to take responsibility for your team when they are near-disengaged. Near-disengaged scores (or as engagement surveys would call, those employees who rated "neutral" in their engagement questions responses) are particularly important to pay attention to, as these scores reflect the people who can open up to being swayed into disengagement, or into engagement.

Engage from Transformative Success versus the Burning Platform

From the many key areas that must always be attended to in an organization, prioritize team engagement through a leadership capacity and capability that focuses on transformative success versus a burning platform focus as a regular practice to engage and achieve results. Transformative success is an approach intended for regular day-to-day practice which focuses on achieving results from purposeful shifts of thinking and habits that align with success – a way of thinking and practicing habits that produce a new level of well-being, capacity, capability, and sustaining results. It is an approach more about building for growth, vitality, and future success. Conversely, with the burning platform focus – a business term used in the approach to emphasize the dire need for immediate, radical change and results due to crisis-based urgencies – the focus is on achieving results. This is not to say that burning platforms don't exist and in certain cases, it's a much-needed approach in the business world today. Take, for instance, General Motors and the recent announcement of plant shut downs, due to economic crisis, in Canada's Oshawa plant and four U.S. plants, planned for December 2019. The rising issue, though, is that urgency has become the norm in many organizations. Each year, organizations introduce lofty targets, cut resources, and expect more with less from their people. This burning platform has become the norm-practice and mentality to how to go about business and getting people to work more and faster. Rather than seeing favourable results, you see exhaustion, toxic relationships, disengagement, mistrust, and strained relationships. Leaders need to ask themselves how many times a burning platform approach really needs to happen before they find their entire workforce exhausted and disengaged. In most cases, better planning, wholistic success focus, better innovative thinking, and proactive measures may very well mitigate from burning platforms becoming the norm. These measures must be considered. Why? Because without these, you can kiss goodbye your dreams for achieving your aligned performance targets, your organization's vision, and sustaining them through a highly-engaged "you" aligned with a highly-engaged team.

I use the term leadership capacity to describe a leader's ability to effectively decide, behave, manage time, and lead themselves and their teams to accomplish the organization's vision and supporting objectives (targets) despite the external forces coming their way. Consequently, a leader exceeds their leadership capacity when they are no longer able to effectively manage or lead themselves and their team to reach the organization's potential. This is also true for team members. When they've reached their capacity to effectively engage from their true purpose in the organization, they are no longer able to effectively tap into their engagement and reach their potential for high results, let alone, the organization's potential. Knowing the whole you (your capacity and engagement) is important to start with so that you know what your next steps are to safeguard from a perfect storm from happening.

Another important point to highlight is that there is a growing number of experts and supporting statistical data which make correlations between leadership capacity and engagement, and the competitive advantage organizations aspire to keep on top of. In North America, we see alarming statistics in mental unwellness at home and at work, the rise of unwellness in the workplace, troubling engagement scores indicating that more balance with life and work is wanted, that people are not feeling connected to the organization, that they don't have enough "this" or enough "that" in the workplace. But what if there is a missing engagement driver that's not connected to the workplace, but at the person level? What if, at the person level, an organization can help and thereby improve engagement?

Many businesses still have significant gaps in the areas of high workplace engagement and leadership capacity which undermine their ability to sustain success. There are many organization-based factors that contribute to these gaps and why they continue to occur. If you have not explored these factors yet, I recommend you learn more about them to give you a sense of the landscape that you are having to lead – what key factors you're facing as relevant to your organization's nuances. There are rich sources for guiding information and research data easily accessible today for deeper reference to help you understand the complexities these factors may have in your organization and how it impacts your role as a leader. Your Human Resources department can also assist you with this, or perhaps you have a management consulting firm that you're already using that can explore this further with you.

Depending on the nature and size of your organization, these impacting factors can include the rise of the multi-generational demographics in the workforce; compensation discrepancies; job and role clarity; clarity of your organization's mission, vision, and values and how these are communicated and translated into everyone's role and performance targets; your organizational culture; expecting more with less resources; human resources systems for talent and performance management; clarity of leadership and management models; decision-making model; accountability clarification; the rise of complexity to meet customer service demands; technology issues; change and transition management; succession planning; competency gaps; wellness practices and needs, and so forth. As you can see, the factors are plenty, complex, and they impact your engagement levels for you and your team.

Your leadership capacity is impacted by these factors too – that is your capacity to make the time for and endure actual leadership work your team, and your organization expect from you. Depending on the effectiveness of your organization's systems to handle issues from any of these factors, you're likely faced with having to personally manage through them which adds to your plate and impacts your own capacity and time. When faced with issues, how do you handle it for yourself, for your team? It starts with determining deep down how you handle thinking about it, what you as leader decide to focus on, what you are willing to do, and what you are capable of when it comes to engagement and your use of time for optimal leadership capacity.

Time and Capacity

As in life, in any organization, time is constant, continual, and irreversible. Once wasted, you can never get that moment in time back. Regardless of position or role, everyone in an organization is susceptible to the truth that they cannot stop time, they cannot slow its pace down, nor can they speed it up. Time has only one direction, to go forward. In every organization, time is needed for constantly hitting targets, for continuous improvements to meet the ever-changing customer/client and competitive demands. This is also the same in other aspects of life. And yet, all too often, whether we know it or not, our thoughts and actions seem to contravene this truth about time. We can find ourselves thinking we can make up the time or rewind it; and then we say, "I just don't have enough time", "I wish I had more time." Rather than focusing on time, focus on what you choose to put into that time and ask yourself if how you spent that time was worthwhile. Reflect on your moments in time – and you'll find that time isn't the issue. This is fundamental for managing and engaging under pressure.

Leaders are charged with a multitude of responsibilities. They are expected to constantly deliver on tasks, projects, and initiatives, to achieve results through their credibility and through their people. Add to that, the layers of strategizing, planning, customer relations, building alliances, and being accountable for inspiring highly engaged team members responsible for achieving productivity and results. And if that wasn't enough, you, the leader, are someone with a personal life that has its own challenges. And so, as a leader, as a person, your in-tray (that tray of "to-do's") is always at full capacity. But how can you juggle all, inspire others to be engaged, and still be effective with all that you are responsible for orchestrating in your whole life? The answer is in what you hold as priority and why and what you're prepared to organize and clarify for yourself and others.

As with every leader, there are many demands coming at you from so many sources vying for your time that you simply cannot afford to waste it. Often, leaders waste time by holding on to habits that no longer work in today's work environment; and when this is not addressed, it only causes a ripple effect to a slew of time-wasters that permeate across the organization.

One key time-waster is tasks that are done but don't serve a clear purpose because there isn't one, and no one ever questions or corrects these. They just get done, maybe for the sake of looking busy, or maybe to pass time because there's no clear sense of direction (purpose).

Another key time-waster I've seen in organizations (regardless of level) is the time spent on complaining and blaming one person or a team, a colleague, a manager, a leader, a "them" against "us". Okay, as a side-bar, I've done this too! Point is, it does not solve anything, it just makes you feel even more miserable and disengaged, which, when you think about it, only worsens whatever it is you were complaining about; and the target you were blaming (if they were confronted) only gets defensive, adding more nasty fuel to the fire. Yes, complaining and blaming is a vicious cycle that wastes precious time and energy, and never achieves anything but more of the same wasteful outcomes.

Another time waster is in whatever constant or habitual chit-chat, social networking or net-surfing going on that has nothing to do with what one was supposed to be focusing on or doing in the first place – you know, that target set for achieving.

Another key time-waster is the marathon meetings that take place that have no purpose to them (need I say more?). John Kenneth Galbraith put it well when he said, "Meetings are a great trap. Soon you find yourself trying to get agreement and then the people who disagree come to think they have a right to be persuaded. However, they are indispensable when you don't want to do anything."

While I suggest the above for your consideration, add to this the consideration of time-wasters you may have existing in your personal life. These are the relationships you keep and how these influence your emotions, thoughts, behaviours, focus, capacity, and engagement level. It's important to be consciously aware of the decisions you make, the relationships you nurture or propagate, the priorities and habits that you choose to fill in your use of time. There may be relationships that trigger you to habits that do not serve your purpose as a leader for your life and for others. Think about it, identify your time-wasters, and choose to take action for eliminating them.

The Prize: Engagement to Success

Sir Richard Branson sums up true success as a state of being, that "the more you're actively and practically engaged, the more successful you will feel." Sharing his sentiments, engagement is all in your feeling during a creative process or journey to achieving what you set out to achieve. It's about that highly focused, euphoric-like feeling you get when you're fully immersed in a situation calling on and allowing you to use your core strengths and connection to purpose. It's when you know you're in your zone of genius, flowing with unusual clarity on where you are, where you want to get to, how to get there. It's when nothing distracts you from this zone and flow. It's about knowing your part in something that has a life of its own, a part of something greater – and you're a part of it from the clarity of your true purpose in that part, sticking with what matters in, and for, that creative flow. It's about feeling pure joy and love for what you are going through because time seems to just stand still when you're in this state. This state is not born from fear and doubt; rather, it's a state coming from love. You feel you can do and achieve all that matters in this state. You know what this state is like – maybe it's when you're playing your favourite sport; or when you're going out for that run at the wee hours of a cold, wet morning; when you're creating an ingenious invention until all hours of the night, despite your early morning start; when you're belting out a song in front of an audience because you feel the brilliant rhythm from your voice and the band; or when you're listening to your favourite music, moving your body spastically to the groove of the beat; or playing an instrument with your eyes shut; or when you're cradling your crying newborn in your arms in the middle of the night for, a fourth time. Or maybe it's when you're in a room with your team, collaborating joyfully on the creation of success you're going to achieve together. Imagine that for you. Imagine that for your team. Imagine – because you truly feel it, believe it and live from it – all of you saying with conviction:

- I am bringing my "whole self" to work
- I am fully engaged at work and in the creative flow for something amazing
- I have hopefulness and a sense of meaning at work because it doesn't feel like work
- I am always creating a feeling of connectedness with my colleagues, my leaders, those I serve
- I am committed to fostering a purpose and mission aligned with what we set out as a team and organization
- I am significantly a part of something amazing
- I belong with my team and larger team
- I am encouraged and supported to feel and achieve work-life balance.

I believe everyone wants this, and for you as a leader, it's critical for you to have this, live by this, to model, support, foster and to promote this as a norm-state for you and your team. Now add to that for you as a leader, making sure that feeling from your team is also constantly being tapped into, and linked to your compelling vision and reasons for what's to be achieved – because they believe you, they believe their part in it, they feel its value to you, to them, and to others, at work and personally.

Your leadership capacity warrants personal answers that only you can answer. Answers for what fuels your inner capacity to handle pressures, how you will address it, as a personal priority for your own engagement level for self, thus permeating out for others. It's not about labeling what you uncover for others, it's about deeply accepting that it's a waste of energy trying to figure out another great leader's characteristic to mold into. You know the job you've been given as a leader. Once that's registered in your mind, you inherently know and trust that committed people working together as a community in the context of love and joy will generate more than you could ever prescribe through a formal strategy. Consider that if you neglect this possibility for truthful answers from within to guide you, you could undermine your duty to serve from the highest version of self within your reach, to connect, in the context of love, joy. This understanding is fundamental for leadership that makes a true difference in a lasting way.

So, remember the great leader profile – it comes with weathering and managing all the good, the bad, the so-so, the great, and the ugly. I'm not proposing that you own your team's engagement source; rather, as a leader, you own influencing the enablement of their engagement – and it starts with understanding your own engagement source and what enables it internally by your thoughts, your beliefs, your passion, your purpose, your focus, and your habits. This will allow you to mitigate the proverbial "leader's perfect storm", while also being able to authentically help others, because you will be able share and lead from a place of love. This begs the question, "How do you know what the right choices are, when all factors and variables coming at you personally and professionally must be addressed and don't always align?" The answer lies in your discovery of and tending to your personal compass, your acceptance as a great leader for your organization, and then basing your choices and actions from that discovery. From this discovery, you will be able to unfold what's needed to cultivate, to nurture and incubate lasting success. There is a way, and this book describes support for your solution approach.

Chapter 2:
VALIDATION

*"Vulnerability is the birthplace
of innovation, creativity and change."*
– Brene Brown

Vulnerability and the Truth

You're not alone in your need to turn your tired and disengaged team around for better results. And you should know that you're also not alone with facing the struggles of managing your time and capacity to handle all that's on your plate in work and in life. You just may think this, causing you anxiety with the notion that you could be exposed as inadequate, so you struggle to armour up and try to hold it all together – you're not alone. For the great leader in you, I want to caution you for being too comfortable in keeping with this company. If you find any comfort in knowing you're not alone with this issue, find comfort only in knowing that it makes you rightly aware that your situation is real and once you tend to it, you can realize the results you're truly after. Resolving this issue starts with you, personally, and solutions are not usually clear cut, even though the path is. It takes ongoing effort, the right mind-set, the right decision-making ability, and the right habits that stick to success.

This personal transformation to success opens you to vulnerability. Embrace this vulnerability, because there is a certain genuineness that comes with it when connected to purpose, clarity and love. I believe that such genuineness models authenticity and is awakened by vulnerability, paving a loving path to deeper connections, and solid relationships that promote growth and vitality in the context of love and joy, not fear. We are all a beautiful work in progress – that's what life is all about, regardless of what circumstance, obstacle, event, role, environment, preoccupy us. Know that whatever it is that you have, right at this very moment – talent, resources, position, challenges, gains, material "stuff," the stuff you think about, they're enough. They're enough to work with to set your success path, authentically. With committing to your personal accountability for thinking, believing, and acting from your true purpose, you will achieve lasting success – and "lasting" is the operative word here. You are also blessed by everything you have in every moment, because you always have choices. I know from experience that you can't gain anything from worrying about what you didn't get, what you don't have, the wrongs that others have imposed on you, fearing risks and obstacles of what's been thrown at you to solve, deal with, whatever. Focus on your power from within and continually fuel it with love – your power to choose what it is you want through and in spite of the pressures before you and in your moments in time. Focus this power to discovering, learning, thinking, believing, and acting from a place of love and true purpose. This power to choose gives you the potential to lead, and it begins on the inside – your head and heart aligned, with awareness, introspection, and acceptance of your highest version of self – your authentic self through which lasting fulfilment of success, for self and for others, is born.

Decisions, Decisions, Dilemmas, Dilemmas

I'm certain you'll agree that life is filled with many dilemmas that we face on a regular basis. Let's take morning routines for example. You could wake up one snow-filled work morning feeling like you want to stay in bed, yet you know there's an important team meeting you're to lead that starts at 9 a.m., and if you stay in bed any longer, you'll likely be late. Do you push that snooze-button for another half-hour with the "sandman" and stay in bed? If you decide to sleep in, you may feel that half-hour was justified, and start thinking about how you'll manage facing peak-traffic on your only route to work. You would rush to get ready, get your kids ready for school, feed them their Froot Loops, and choose to skip breakfast for yourself, even though you know you'll likely not have time for lunch because of the meeting. You get into your car and you know you must get to the office as quickly as possible, but safely. To get there, you must decide your best route and speed to keep so you're not late. To maintain safety in getting there you must manoeuvre through the flow of traffic, watch for the fastest lane moving, ensuring safety and getting to your destination on time. Decisions you make in this scenario are potentially contradictory – and are dilemmas.

According to the Oxford dictionary, the definition of dilemma is "a situation in which a difficult choice has to be made between two or more alternatives, especially ones that are equally undesirable." In organizations, dilemmas surface all the time. You have those dilemmas your boss or HR talks about when they say, "You're in charge as the leader, but make sure your team is on board and given what they need to keep them engaged. Now go get those results for us."

Core Dilemmas (Personal Level)

Of the various factors that lead to mistakes in decision making, I've learned that one of the most powerful is personal attachments – to people, to places, to the past, to fears of exposure, loss, and not pleasing others, to personal habits, and to things. While these attachments may serve value when linked with true purpose (for awareness and care of safeguarding what's really important to you), many times, these attachments cause us to give in to our raw emotions such as anger, hurt, or apathy, and that's when these attachments push us into potential issues for achieving what we truly want, because we get stuck.

Take Jonathan for example. He was a second-generation owner who after six years of running his father's business, contacted me for help with his disengaged team. At our initial consultation, he seemed pretty clear about the source of his issue: that his 50 employees were not meeting the targets he'd set for two consecutive years and he needed to fix it because they were, after all, the long-standing experts to the business during his dad's reign. But he didn't know how to fix this.

After gathering more information around his business, we determined a workable three-year plan for re-engaging his staff through a skills inventory exercise, team building, and involvement strategy for business growth through a new line of business. During the first few months, I noticed that he was regularly not available at the office. His absence from the office grew more frequent, and after validation from staff that this was a regular occurrence (golfing, long lunches, vacations, etc.) I set up a meeting with him to discuss this. What I learned was that he wasn't interested in leading a large team and was himself tired of the business altogether but knew that it was the only business he knew he could do and get a lofty income from (not to mention that it was a pretty sweet inheritance to receive the guaranteed job as CEO). We spent time fleshing this out through deeper personal exploratory discussions of what he truly wanted out of the business and for the business. We also spent time exploring his personal struggles and needs. I proposed to him that it was possible to change his strategy to one that more aligns with his passions and core needs (true purpose). My remaining time with him was focused on his self-discovery and transformation journey and streamlining his business to meet what he'd discovered about himself and his vision.

After two years of dedicating to the new business transformation strategy and his personal development and mindset, he realized the success he was really wanting, and continues to be one of the leading and long-standing services company in his field. He remains proud to carry on the business legacy for his parents, with his renewed business vision being realized. This example demonstrates how great ventures are found out of passion and to let go of the attachment to things that deviate from that passion and authenticity – things such as entitlement or externally-driven expectations contrary to the self. If you don't have your own passion, you don't care. If you don't care, you don't attain meaningful success that sustains and permeates out.

Dilemmas and decisions are first managed from within. Those dilemmas come with pressures that impose on how you will react and respond to them for the sake of being a great leader. These pressures cannot be delegated for someone else to figure out in terms of how you will deal with them, because figuring it out lies in your mindset. When your mindset is not focused on the right things to consider and the right thoughts and beliefs to align with that focus, these pressures can strain your leadership capacity as I described in the previous chapter.

You know when you've just ended a work week and you can't wait for your weekend to begin? That frantic Monday has come and gone and you're thankful for the Friday when you can exhale and say, "Thank God this week is over". You barely remember the moments of the week that made you smile, but you're excited – excited by the thought of turning off your brain, even just for a few hours, and letting go of a draining week. Saturday entails the hopeful squeeze in for a bit of a sleep in. But you know it well, that jolt from the flurry of worries circling in your head that wakes you. You no longer need an alarm clock because life as you know it blasts you to solider up for your day's predictable full schedule of fitting in that time you need or felt guilt over for having barely shared with loved ones, for the necessary household chores, errands, and leadership dilemmas to plan and strategize for. If you haven't made time for your work, you take the Sunday for that, maybe after a quick time-in with your loved ones and once you've driven the kids around, picked up groceries, tackled the laundry pile, already responding to work emails that popped up on your mobile phone since Friday night. And then it begins – the stewing Sunday blues that boil over into panic before you tuck in for another restless night. You've felt your brain progressively racing, your breath becoming shallow, and your energy dwindled at an all-time low because you know the busy-ness and problems to solve are just around the corner. You know what awaits you: all things needed to be accomplished and solved in the new week, with and through your team that's just as tired and disengaged as you are.

Monday morning of the new workweek. You've done this before, and you wish you could have just one more day off. You feel overwhelmed, stressed and you haven't even begun your day. The moment you get into the office you're already drained by entering what you're certain will continue to play out in the week: marathon meetings; problems to lead through; people to inspire; issues to mediate; futile attempts to meet others' needs; the politics of business. At day's end, you find yourself back at it, bringing work home because of the fire-fighting and issues that have yet to be resolved. Your time for loved ones goes by the way-side yet again, and you motion that clock-work bare bones home-rou-tine just to get it out of the way so you can get back to work later that evening. And yes, another restless night. Does this sound familiar?

If so, here's the reality. Many find themselves in this energy-zap-ping timetable predicament that impacts their capacity, their ability to find balance, to love their moments, to make the right decisions and act from authenticity and purpose as a great leader, their purpose as whole person, for themselves and for others. There is a way to start clearing your path through this chaos. This way comes from within you, and when tapped, it rejuvenates, it puts balance first, it grounds you, so that you can make a difference for achieving lasting results you and others can be proud of, through your leadership.

Core Dilemmas (Organizational Level)

In an organization, yes, dilemmas exist no matter what, and it's a leader's role to ensure they're effectively managed. To help, there are supports usually considered such as HR, Legal counsel or a core team that focuses on governance matters developing those business-ethical operating policies and procedures (e.g., financial regulatory, human resources policies, codes of conduct, reporting breaches, suspicious behaviour and conduct that materially harm the organization or its people, public, and clients, etc.). When enterprise-wide change mandates are planned for, these guidelines, along with project-focused meetings are usually set in motion to ensure dilemmas and decisions are well informed and planned for implementation. But what if, at the personal leadership level, leaders haven't prepared themselves for their capacity to make right decisions? What seems to be missing, is the regular ongoing support for dealing with matters where ambiguity exists, calling for a leader to draw from within (their mindset, heart, emotional capability and intelligence) for the right solutions, and not merely through a policy.

From my time at CIBC, I worked under the HR leadership that created The Leadership Centre which I believe started CIBC's mark as one of the leading learning organizations. During this time, I learned from Hubert Saint-Onge, the conceptual creator of the Centre's strategic leader, (senior VP of strategic capabilities at the time), and his research finding that for the organization there were at least nine core leadership dilemmas leader face, causing pressures that have a domino effect with sustaining personal and team engagement. When I work with my clients, and adding to Saint-Onge's findings, I have found that the following ten core dilemmas come up offering insights about the pressures that leaders face and must be ready for, in an emotionally intelligent and resilient manner:

Core Dilemma 1: Enterprise-wide leadership versus high-visibility (presence) leadership

Core Dilemma 2: Independence versus Cross-boundary/Inter- or Intra-dependence

Core Dilemma 3: Long-term focus versus Short-term focus (important versus urgent)

Core Dilemma 4: Creativity versus Discipline and Directives

Core Dilemma 5: Trust versus Change and Transition Management

Core Dilemma 6: Hierarchical Decision-making versus Flat-structure Decision-making

Core Dilemma 7: People Growth and Personal Transformative Development versus Productivity Growth

Core Dilemma 8: Authenticity versus Alignment

Core Dilemma 9: Leadership versus Capability

Core Dilemma 10: Return on Investment (ROI)/Revenue Growth versus Cost Containment

From Saint-Onge's findings, and as highlighted in Fortune Magazine (March 18, 1996), he was reported to highlight that "…they form a single, central dilemma…the never-ending balancing act in which you try to give people independence and authority while making sure they use it in a way you'd approve of if they asked, which you don't want them to do except, of course, when you do want them to." Core dilemmas in organizations, in life, exist and continually test the leader's limits for decision-making, and aligning engagement at the core self-level.

A Case of Realizing and the Brain at Work

A few years ago, I worked with a great leader whose business was going through a transformation which he had gained approval for – the plan and vision was established by him, yet, he admitted that he was overwhelmed with what was happening around him when it came to the workforce. He logically understood the value for centralizing multiple sites into one larger site; but did not know how to address the human resources (the people) issues. Each site specialized in a service to the same client. He knew that each of the sites had their own way of doing things to "serve" the client and a centralization in their minds was, well, not a comfortable concept because it meant change in doing things. He indicated feeling overwhelmed by not knowing how to lead the "people" issues. After a few strategy discussions with him, he admitted that he was concerned about his capacity and capability to lead this aspect of the business restructure and that his key high-potential team members could start becoming disengaged. He speculated they probably already were disengaged (or near it) from the spike in absence rates, the low morale bubbling from the news of the centralization, and the low scores of client satisfaction target rates. He feared this disengagement from team members would cause resignations or an increase in disgruntled staff, unless something different was done. I recognized this feeling from leaders of other organizations whom I've helped. I appreciate this leader for recognizing this about his own capacity and capability. That realization was like an insurance policy against his leadership failing. He committed to engaging me to help, both as his lead for the HR stream of the centralization, and as his personal leadership coach for helping him rejuvenate his own engagement, focus and productivity for results that served the vision. After a year and a half of working with him to understand his business, guiding him through the complexities and source issues he needed to address, including his personal leadership capacity for re-engaging himself and turning around a resistant team, he successfully centralized the organization with a renewed leadership strategy and approach he felt personally capable to carry out. This gained him the added value of attaining the highest engagement score in his region-sector for four consecutive years, creating an inclusive and cross-collaborative work environment across the inter- and intra- professional roles.

Through the years of working closely with him, there were a few key points of aha's worth highlighting. The first aha was that this leader was also going through a marriage break up during the business restructure implementation, and rather than dealing with his raw emotions about it, he dove right into his work. In fact, he realized that it wasn't until the emotional aspects of the business transition started to rise, that his own personal issues started surfacing for him, causing him to struggle with making decisions around the workforce. Another aha was that he referred to me as his "right brain" because he insisted that he was "left-brain through and through." He felt secure with this. In truth, from my experience, we use both sides of our brain. Recent articles in pop-psychology and neuroscience also demonstrate that while we may be left-brain or right-brain dominant, both sides are at play and there's a whole other brain component that connects it all together. The general theory around right-brain and left-brain is in what each side typically brings out from a thinking perspective. The theory claims right-brain refers to the side of your brain that synthesizes, fosters intuitiveness, subjectivity, creativity, imagination, artistry, and sees the whole picture. The left-brain refers to the side of your brain that fosters rationalization, objectivity, and language recognition, brings logic, and organizes.

Then there's this neocortex part of our brain, the most advanced part that controls it all, which has two sides which determine how we think. I confess that getting into it beyond this notion, while fascinating, gives me a headache as I'm not an expert on neuroscience at all. What I have taken from this, however, ("left-brain" thinking perspective at play here), is that there's validity to how our entire brain plays out to how we think, manage our emotions, and base our decisions and behaviours from it. The truly exciting thing is that this can be leveraged to your leadership advantage.

Self-Realization at Work

Geri, a client of mine, knew she had to make some decisions about her newly acquired team who were showing signs of disengagement after they had experienced recent changes in their work area. She was concerned about the upcoming new lofty targets she would be rolling out to them. It kept her up at nights and left her overwhelmed for the last three months since taking on her new appointment as vice president. She oversaw a division that spanned across 26 sites across Ontario. She remembered fondly her recent success with having led a previous division within the same organization. She recalled how it was smooth sailing back then, and for the eight years she led that team, she was proud of them and the accomplishments they achieved together. In her new appointment, she wondered if she'd ever get to a point of the same level of high engagement she recalled from her last team. In the years, the organization had gone through its changes and challenges and this new portfolio faced the brunt of it, leaving everyone in this portfolio exhausted and skeptical of hope for anything but more targets, more tiring work, more changes, more to do with less people. What made matters worse for this team was that they were spread out across multiple locations, not under one facility as was the last team Gerri led. Spread out across multiples site locations, the feeling of being one team seemed impossible to grasp for them, and according to Gerri, the hope for her being able to make a difference for them seemed bleak.

When Gerri contracted me for coaching support, she mentioned that she had an executive coach assigned to her already. Curious, I asked her if there was a reason that stood out for why she felt she needed yet another coach. Her response was, "I think there are personal issues I'm having, and I need help to sort them out without getting overwhelmed with the business-side coaching I'm getting." This is another example of a personal realization of that insurance policy against leadership failing. We started our engagement, and through her committed work, my coaching support, and the safe space I could offer her, we were able to uncover key elements to what she needed to explore – foundational items such as what drives her; what experiences made her grow to being a leader and become engaged; her habits, focus, will and capability for supporting others; her fundamental core beliefs about people, work, life; her current state with feeling present with others; what she knows about herself and her relationship with self; her attachments to the past; the relationships she keeps; her aspirations personally and professionally; her true purpose, core values, joys, needs and wants. And more.

The biggest value for Gerri has been that she was able to uncover her biggest time-wasters: worrying about things and putting important things off, which led to much of her indecisiveness to take actions that stuck to what she felt was successful; creating inefficiency rather than mitigating it; constantly welcoming unanticipated interruptions that did not have meaningful purpose for her true self and core genius; procrastinating; overcommitments; excessive involvement with crisis management; attending meetings without clarity of purpose; failing to delegate; poor planning; lack of clarity for directions; too many priorities with limited understanding of meaningful value; too many time management systems; limited standards (lots of ad hoc matters). Today, she is seeing the positive results accelerating as she feels renewed after gaining a clear vision for how to approach engagement as a person so that she can be a great leader. She even finds time she once imagined impossible to focus on what truly matters personally and professionally. She and her team are starting to feel rejuvenated as they collaborate on their path to achieve their aligned results with meaningful success.

Measure of Leadership Effectiveness

Stephen R. Covey once said, "Effective leadership is putting first things first. Effective management is discipline, carrying it out." This has stuck with me in the years. Consequently, when focus is on external results and gains, it's easy to get caught up on incessant 'doing' without a clear focus for what's really important, and this can become the norm, resulting in a style of management where focus is aligned to a need for controlling outputs rather than valuing success' true source: passion and purpose from each person and their unique value, which is driven from love and joy. Managing by control can lead to being available for everything, including frivolous, and meaningless tasks that cause us to lose our way from the essence of why we do and acquire things in the first place. As a result, our very essence (love, joy, passion, and purpose) for what unleashes the exceptional is diluted for the sake of doing and being under unnecessary pressure. When this happens, we find ourselves yearning for more time, questioning our capability and capacity, wondering what the meaning is behind it all. We end up pining for an effective solution or system to deal with our use of time just to take on more, or maybe we blame or complain about others getting in our way, all the while needing to inspire them to help us. If this rings true to you, perhaps you can relate to the resulting symptoms of excessive focus on success borne from the externally-driven need for perfection and related performance: fatigue, anxiety, depression, sleeplessness, guilt, binging, loss of appetite, incessant frustration, control, obsessiveness, competitiveness, insatiability, inertia, craving for more time, help and balance, and feeling overwhelmed from it all.

Regardless of role and environment (personal or professional) many of us accept the demands for producing, relating, and performing for the sake of others' standards, for the recognizable external status we believe we can gain from the roles we take on. While these pressures may be deemed as necessary, they will likely take you down the path of unnecessary added pressures, compounding to an overload of resulting issues because we no longer have the capacity to carry on with the never-ending full and overlapping schedule of 'to do's'.

Where does this net us? Aside from the painful symptoms highlighted earlier, it can likely net us to the nagging whispers that one day demand answers from us: at what price and why? Is it worth it? Consequently, when these pressures have no clear alignment with what you truly believe, the answers are manifested into a reality that can be quite rude and painful: exhaustion; missed time with loved ones; missed commitments; lack-luster in our moments; a busy mind that can't make decisions, yet wanting to control; fatigue; pretending all is fine and dandy, but not really – just to appear we've got our act together.

I know it all too well from the early years of my career. I had layered, one on top of the other, a multitude of roles seemingly of equal importance, as my measure for success was by everyone's standard but my own: best daughter, best mom, best sibling, best worker, best student, best manager, best consultant, best coach, best caregiver, best friend, best aunt, best volunteer, and so on. I lost track of the very essence for why these roles were important to me in the first place – and God forbid I miss my performance in any of them. I became so foreign to my own self. I was wrought with tremendous guilt whenever one role swallowed my time over another role. My roles, and achieving in them, became my identity.

I found that if I produced below the expected standards in any of them, I was not relevant for others, and it was all my fault – like socks becoming useless from when you can't find one, of the pair, on the morning you find yourself late for an important meeting. Darn sock! So, what do I do? I overbook my time, work harder and longer hours because that was simpler than dealing with my secret of feeling unworthy, and void, in my mind. I completely dismissed the nag of what it was I needed, including what I secretly craved which was balance for feeling present and feeling the love of my moments with myself, with my family, friends, others.

Deep down, fear drove me. Fear from being found out as a big fake by everyone else's standards, my self-shame grew. That was my routine way for a few years. In those years, everything progressively became a chore, an overwhelming schedule of commuting, producing for work, leaving me too exhausted to love anything outside of work routines. I may have achieved my target of earning that six-figure income, but with it, came those whispers for answers from the heart. I was unravelling fast and could no longer keep up, as evident from my bouts of crying in my pillow over nothing; my sleepless nights; burning the midnight oil for work all the while wishing I could win the lottery; my growing obsessive low tolerance and high irritation for every little thing that could go wrong (even that darn sock I keep losing!); guilt for little personal and family time; not knowing how to say no to work deadlines; insatiable binges of food, drink, social. I grew to hate my life secretly. Add to that, a failed marriage, which threw me into a brutal child custody battle (are they ever anything but brutal, really?) and into finding a new house to call home.

A final straw that literally broke me was the eventual onset of three autoimmune diseases that depleted my energy level and forced me to live at a slower pace: SLE Lupus, Sjogrens, and Primary Biliary Cirrhosis. I remember the early days of my diagnoses. The mix of progressive pains and aches with a cocktail of medications that made me loopy and more absent-minded than normal. I grew more ashamed of myself, so I hid it through more work and over-doing. There was no time for mourning my lost energy and dreams, so I thought. I had bills to pay, a household to maintain with a single income, and growing teen with, well, you know. I took my prescriptions and sucked it all up as I carried on with my militant regimen of performing and producing like a happy, loving widget-maker for a life to which I became a slave.

Whenever things did not go according to the routines and schedules I depended on for achieving the performance of my roles, it would send me to the depths of chaos, anxiety, guilt, shame, blame, self-victimization, self-righteousness, incessant 'doing', self-loathing and worthlessness, clinging on to the masks of each role I did well to perform for everyone, until I woke up and found an empty shell I could no longer ignore. And then I crashed, to the point of forced surrender which involuntarily came in the form of three significant breakdowns in my life. They led me to therapy counselling and personal transformation programs such as Landmark and The Bob Hoffman Institute. Somehow, through these crash events which I call my "blessings in disguise," I found time for myself through dedicated personal transformation development – a path that changed my level of performance in life and career, for the better and from the inside, out.

Today and for the last 13 years, I'm still faced with the dilemmas and challenges, but my life's path is centered on my true purpose. I am loving my present moments and those around me. I am engaged with my deliberate design of a meaningful life I want, for myself and to contribute in the world from my core purpose, passion, love, and joy. Unlike before, I can feel I am on a fulfilling lifestyle and thriving business-track that meets my purpose for each day's moments. I can clearly recognize my capability, my capacity, my limitations and my potential for continuously refining my journey toward my next goals. I feel centered, successful by my standards and focused. Sure, I have my human moments of emotional bouts, yet now, I can accept myself and bounce back more quickly from knowing what I want and how I will get there. I feel my loving, remarkable path to level up my place in helping others to achieve the same authentic success, but in their own way and through essentials for lasting success and greater possibilities for self and others.

What I grew to cathartically realize through my experience (and continue to) was that the measure of aspired external success was the very thing causing my internal demise: success aspired from being "best" for others, but never paying attention to feeling and being better from the inside out. I was so busy worrying about whether I fit in to external standards that it sent me in a tizzy. I did not know what to do first, so I did everything all at once, without clarity of my own compass. I couldn't figure out who I lovingly was in anything I did for myself or others. I just kept doing, pining, and beating myself up, beating life up.

Authentic Purpose and Passion

I will never forget my experience with one of the big five banks in Canada, the Canadian Imperial Bank of Commerce (CIBC) which kick-started my true passion for personal leadership and authentic success transformation. My experience with CIBC offered me a clear path to nurture my personal goal for a career in Human Resources (HR); and it opened my heart to clarify my deep passion for one day being able to share learnings of the value of personal leadership transformation for wholistic success. I wonder if I would be where I am today if it had not been for this experience.

CIBC was the organization that took a chance on me to start my HR career. I began with them in 1992 as a resourcing consultant for what is known today as Capital Markets (back then, they were two distinct entities, Investment Banking and Private Clients, Wood Gundy). After literally hundreds of recruitment projects under my belt, collaborating with a large Human Resources department responsible for an excess of 6,000 employees, nationwide, for traders, brokers, mid and senior management, employees, and prospective candidates, I then entered two other subsidiaries over a six-year period, payment processing and e-commerce, which had me traveling to northern California, New York City, Colorado, and Florida. My career in Human Resources progressed rapidly during these years as I went from working recruitment to employee relations and human resources business partnering. What sticks with me the most from this near-decade experience is the people, relationships gained with them, and the dynamic creative brilliance I was exposed to because of them during that time. I was bright-eyed and bushy-tailed for developing that right career and passion path.

Al Flood was the CEO and Chairman of CIBC during much of my tenure and what resonated with me during my time under his reign was the bold rollout of leadership development throughout all levels of the organization, led by Human Resources leader Michelle Darling. By 1994, a significant investment was made toward building and launching a leadership centre dedicated to the organization's leaders and high-potential employees. It would be located just 45 minutes north of CIBC's head office in Toronto, Ontario. There was much that went into ensuring its mandate, management, success, and measurement of return on investment. This facility was based in King City, Ontario, set on a rolling 100-acre backdrop. It became the wellness-type retreat centre that offered time and rich learning for personal leadership development and transformation. Looking back on my experience with this program (The Foundations of Leadership), I can't help but to believe that it was one of the most significant base-points for shaping my life approach to success, even though I didn't know it at the time. I believe it was also significant for CIBC's paradigm shift to success management through a wholistic personal leadership approach, a movement within the marketplace that was growing to be the "way" to engagement. Following the successors for Al and Michelle, CIBC continues to achieve accolades as a leading organization for its learning culture and leadership development dedication.

From this leadership development program, I learned that when every key aspect of an individual's inner work is paid attention to and given a workout – mental, emotional, physical, and spiritual – it can lead the individual to feeling a sense of belonging from a place of trust and support; and as though anything they desire for progress is possible for them to achieve.

The program introduced me to the Franklin-Covey curriculum which focused on the timeless principles and habits for authentic personal leadership, interpersonal relationships, and time management. This led me to continuing my transformative learning with the likes of Robin Sharma, and Jack Canfield's Success Principles, years after my time at CIBC. Much of my learning from these experiences have been woven into how I approach my life and how I guide others in their own self-awareness, personal and mindset transformation journey today.

Sharpening the Saw – for Heart, Mind, and Arms Wide Open

When I continued my transformative personal leadership development work following my years at CIBC, I continued to diversify and grow my HR skills and expertise across different sectors, with the goal of eventually running my own HR consulting practice. What I learned in those years is that the ongoing focus and dedication to transformative education and development in personal growth provides a solid basis for the required inner leadership it takes to solve problems, identify solution-based opportunities within problems. Within five years of leaving employment, I opened up my own consulting and coaching business which continues to allow me the opportunity to help others progress in the context of love and joy.

Three pivotal influences for me were Bob Hoffman's Hoffman Process, Stephen R. Covey's timeless insights and teachings of principle-centred leadership and success habits, and Jack Canfield's reinforcement of these insights and teachings, within his own pragmatic insights, teachings, and methodology for implementing the power of focus through success principles, of which I am certified to train and teach. As I continue to apply these learned practices in my own life, I share them today with my clients, because, well, they are engrained in me, my passion, and purpose.

I believe that all true success starts from within the self, allowing passion and purpose to express itself in all of life's opportunities for that expression. Until you can personally work out all that keeps you from reaching and realizing your full potential, there will be chaos that clouds you and the results you are trying to achieve.

The Key to Your Own Success

The surest path to reaching high engagement and achieving the highest results in an organization happens one person at a time, and it starts with you. I'm talking, the authentic you, before the layers of life cloaked you, before you became a leader for your organization. I propose exploring how those layers feel for you; how they serve the authentic you; what to do about your discovery as it relates to where you are personally and what you want to achieve in present day. What can guide you is practicing a framework that starts from the beginning with your end in mind, and continually addressing your conscious deliberate design of how you respond to circumstances, to your moments because your response serves your true purpose from your authentic self.

By uncovering your authentic self, you not only improve your experience in life and work, you also enhance your positive influence and servitude of those around you. In fact, through this, you can enhance the motivation, morale, and performance of your team through learned approaches. Such approaches include connecting others to their sense of authentic identity and self to their work and collective identity to the organization; being a role model for your team in order to inspire and enable their engagement from their core genius (talents and skills); challenging them to take greater ownership for their work and outputs, and understanding their strengths and growth needs, allowing you to align them to tasks that enhance their performance.

Recent studies about emerging organization cultures show that there is a powerful call for change coming from the middle leadership ranks of an organization (vice-president, director, senior manager, manager) and reaching out to the critical mass. This call for change comes from a growing consciousness that we are seeing more and more in the workplace. It's a conscious awareness that deep down, things just don't align for individuals, including the leader. A conscious awareness that's about feeling whole in the workplace, not feeling pulled in every direction. It's about having a sense of balance and a euphoric flow so that you can do meaningful work that serves a compelling purpose and achieves lasting results.

I believe that with the right and personalized solution-path, we all can create more steady footing for our own capacity to experience true engagement in life and in the workplace. Whenever we raise our awareness and consciousness to this and commit to our true self – our authenticity and core genius – we not only shift the trajectory of all that is greatly possible for our own life, we positively affect those around us.

Critical Mass Healing

It is mission critical for you to address the inner elements of your own personal leadership capacity issues as it relates to your external elements affecting you – I refer to this as an inside-out approach. By doing this, you'll be able to turn around your tired and disengaged team. It is mission critical for you to refocus your use of time to ensure your transformation for success is top priority for you. Otherwise, you will likely not achieve lasting balance for yourself as you will continue to spin your wheels. If not prioritized, you could undermine your right as a great leader. You risk low productivity, high turnover, more work on your plate, no time for leading your team and those that matter to you, limiting your capacity to perform from core genius. The result, you and your team continuing to be tired and feeling less than energetic, less than productive.

By addressing your leadership capacity and engagement from the inside-out, imagine what could be, what you could enable the workplace that allows for the following:

- Increased synergy, job performance and productivity
- Reduced stress (those stresses that are useless, and time-wasters!)
- Improved team relationships
- A greater climate of trust
- Greater job satisfaction, engagement, and personal well-being
- An intrinsic sense of balance
- Greater commitment to the organization through the fostering of a purpose and mission aligned with the spirit of your team members (that includes you)

It is important to remind yourself that there will never be a free moment to put time into leadership activities unless you choose to make the time. If you wait for a time when everything else is done, that may very well be all you get, moments of waiting. Identify and commit to the moments in time for your personal transformation, incorporate it into your leadership schedule, set and practice habits that serve true purpose, and model it to encourage others to do same for themselves. A young director, highly regarded by his organization said to me, "I know that once in a while, I'll get a talking to for pushing back on some requests from my boss, but in the big picture, the benefit of putting time into developing myself for my team far outweighs the cost." The expression "a talking to" seems apropos because it implies a check-in acknowledgement, but not a major reprisal. The world doesn't end, and we can manage to put more moments of time into leadership.

The time is now to start. To start, you need to identify and address the gap between where you are now (current) and where you want to be (desired end state). Once the gap (and its elements, including the inner elements) is identified it can be addressed, and you will find the solution path to take – and guess what, it starts with understanding yourself deep down for what you own for the only things you can control: your thoughts, behaviour/ attitude, and mental images – your mindset.

Imagine this, your stewing Sunday blues turns into serene Sunday. Your manic Monday turns to motivated Monday because all is well, from within. A clear solution path for authentic success exists for you because of your choice for prioritizing self-awareness and discovery of all within your essence. You have razor-sharp focus because you have clarity of this path and its wholistic purpose. You are clear and you take action from that clarity because you live your life by design and not by default.

Stephen R. Covey reminds us that people are people, regardless of role, environment, and related demands. He also reminds us that, "we must never be too busy sawing, to take time to sharpen the saw," that we must know what our "big rocks" (the things that really matter) are and prioritize them when managing our use of time, leading results through the authentic you so that we can lead and inspire others from this authenticity. So, leading effectively, starts with you and how you lead your life through what you decide, what you choose as those "big rocks." Many fill their jar of life with pebbles, even sand. What do you fill your jar with?

Chapter 3:

THE **FACTOR** FRAMEWORK

"If you follow someone else's way,
you are not going to realize your potential."
– Joseph Campbell, *The Hero's Journey*

Prelude

Helping yourself first is essential to helping others in a massive way. Think of that safety orientation the flight attendant gives just before the plane takes off – you put your oxygen mask on first, and then help others with theirs. It's the same for leading people in an organization. Those dilemmas and pressures that fill your leadership timetable, they require something only you can control, sharpen and be ready to draw from, to stand up to them: your mindset, your focus, your core genius, your habits. With that, ask yourself "what kind of help do I need?" There is a framework you can use to help guide you – a framework I call FACTOR. This framework can help your capacity and capability to re-engage yourself and others so that it produces the results you want.

Oh-pen, the Possibilities!

To achieve something you really want, before you can do so, you must first be open to possibilities for the great things you can achieve. By being open, you allow yourself to refine your focus and connect to what it takes achieve what you want. When you commit, you accept no excuses, you accept only results and the way to those results. Now, to be clear, I'm talking about the kind of openness that you see when you've imagined winning the lottery for $60 Million and what great things you'll do with it, so you buy the ticket. Or the kind of openness as if you've accepted an invitation from a childhood best friend you haven't seen or heard from in years, and you've imagined the reconnect couldn't possibly be anything less than what you expect when you see your best buddies. How open are you to the possibilities? When you feel positively intrigued, curious, and hopeful, because you can imagine the great outcome this possibility could give you, you will align with being completely open. I have found from my own experience, and that of some of my clients', that necessity often takes you to a place of openness. Open yourself to the possibility that if you make even a slight change in the context of love and joy, you could set the stage for significant achievement, and even discover greater fulfillment. As Pablo Picasso once said of his own openness, "Others have seen what is and asked why. I have seen what could be and asked why not."

There was a man named Noah McVicker from Cincinnati Ohio who, in the 1930's invented this non-toxic goo for Kutol, a soap manufacturer he worked at. This goo was created on a request by Kroger grocer representatives for a wallpaper cleaning solution to sell in their stores. At the time, wallpaper cleaners were in huge demand since burning coal was the only means to cheaply and more efficiently heat homes than wood. A negative side effect to coal-burning was that it left coal residue on homeowners' wallpapered walls and water-based solutions did not work for cleaning off the coal residue. According to sources, Noah's invention led to 15,000 cases of this wallpaper cleaning product.

For about a decade, Kutol made incredible profit from this invention. Unfortunately, after World War II, manufacturing companies developed a vinyl wallpaper, which caused sales to plummet for this cleaning product, and so this massive non-toxic goo was left by the wayside, eventually unsellable. By the 1950's, an extraordinary thing happened for this goo. Noah's nephew, Joseph McVicker (who also worked for the soap manufacturer) received a call from his sister-in-law, a nursery school teacher named Kay Zufall. Kay had read an article in the local newspaper about how this wallpaper goo was being recommended as a cost-efficient tool for art projects and urged Noah and Joseph to remake and market the goo as a toy putty for children. With trade secret refinements made for child-safety, pliability, colour, and a distinctive scent that remind many of us of our joyful childhood, they created the first children's toy putty, with Joseph giving it its name: Play-Doh. To date, this invention has resulted in over seven hundred million pounds of Play-Doh sold. Four small tins of Play-Doh sit on my shelf within easy reach to this day. In fact, I'm playing with one right now– the blue one as I write with this book. As I mold it through my fingers, I can smell its scent and I'm brought back to my playful creative self, when I had everything and all that I needed to know, to feel love and joy for that moment. I'm also reminded of Carl Jung's wisdom that "The Artist [in us] connects with us with superhuman and timeless worlds beyond our conscious knowing." I use this Play-Doh story (and playing with it) throughout my coaching framework, to remind myself and my clients that we are always one small adjustment away from creating our lives to make it brilliant.

Use this book as a guide to how to go about achieving success through your discovery and nurturance of your authentic self. Through your authentic self, you will be able to access your true source for lasting success – one which paves way to feeling purposeful, finding meaning and clarity, feeling balanced and recognized for your leadership that makes a true difference.

Enter Your Journey

Now that you're open, make a choice for how you will go about setting and acting on your direction. If you're reading this book, and you've gotten to this page, choose to read on so you can start your journey to the solution and achieving what you want. This is your journey toward authentic success – to eliminating the chaos you're feeling inside you because of your situation and all emotions that consequently come up for you that get in the way of you achieving your external success. Success is really all about getting from your current state/situation to your desired state/situation, and the experience and refinements that are within that journey. Simply put, it's getting from point A to point B, and dealing with all of what's in between so you can break through to your point B. The journey involves finding out, with razor-sharp clarity, what your current state/situation is (Point A), what your desired state/situation is (Point B), what the gap is between A and B, identifying what needs to be addressed in that gap, identifying the actions and plan to addressing those gaps, and then taking action.

In the next several chapters, I demonstrate a framework that can be used to help you transform for success, from the inside-out – accepting things as they are, accepting yourself as you are, and from there going about your transformation and actions for success, which in turn, unfolds to external results beyond your current thinking for exceptional possibilities.

Framework Summary

Generally, a framework is a conceptual structure which serves as a guiding support for building that which is aimed to expand such a structure into something meaningful. Having a framework helps to find a path that's right for you – a path that will lead you to what you uncover as the right direction toward your "end in mind." For clarification, then, a framework does not replace the true source for determining a person's path – or "way." Your "way" is yours.

F.A.C.T.O.R.

The 6-phases of the FACTOR framework have supporting processes and steps that guide that phase. The phases are intended to be integrative, iterative of each other, and how each is applied and focused on depends on the individual's unique needs.

We have setbacks and sometimes we just need a tune-up reminder that this is a normal part of progressing through life. How we respond to those challenges determines if we will go through a downward spiral, if we will become stagnant, or if we will progress, grow, and develop. From my own experience and that of my clients, we can often expect or hope progress to be linear, clear cut, and prescriptive. On the contrary, the tendency is that we make progress, experience setbacks, learn from it, recover, experience something new, experience setbacks again, recover, and then make progress again – and so begins the iteration. Hence, the phases are integrative and iterative in nature to ensure we can efficiently pull from each phase what we need for wherever we find ourselves in our journey.

After having gone through many transformation programs, analyzing hundreds of books, and taking success management courses that have made a difference for me and for others I share learnings and teachings with, I've discovered they all share similar attributes and principles of success. Woven into my framework are time-tested principles and key habits for authentic success pulled from those who have become some of my most favourite teachers in the field of success management, personal, and mindset transformation. On discovering the principles and habits, I realized, though clumsily, that I had been practicing many of them throughout my own life, long before I came across the teachings from the experts. I've used what I've learned to refine my approach to life personally as well as in my career of helping others in workplaces and in their own personal lives. These principles and habits are not new, yet timeless and universal with their effectiveness.

In later chapters, you'll come to realize I touch up on key principles and habits woven into the essential fabric of my framework, focusing on how you can be guided to resolve your personal issues stemming from your pressures to perform, motivate, engage, and sustain aligned results.

My framework's fundamental purpose is to help you identify key personal elements within your gap between your current state and desired state, to help you determine what you choose to personally address to bridge the gap to authentic success.

F – Framing the Foundation for Your Success

Building your frame for your desired outcomes allows you to begin with the end in mind, the current state you are in, and the issues that are getting in the way of your end in mind, clearly defined. Your frame addresses the navigation system that gets you to the quickest and most meaningful means, as it also addresses the gap between your current state and future desired state (your vision) – those issues that are getting in the way. This frame ensures support through the personal dimensions of what you will need to draw from to effectively respond to pressures and demands. This section also focuses on the essentials for setting the right foundational mindset for your solution path to achieve success and making it last.

A – Actions That Stick to Success

Acting on what we set out to do, knowing what to act on, when and how, is critical for achieving success in anything; otherwise what you want stays a dream, or wishful thinking. Take, for instance, the 1954 famous painting by Mark Rothko, "No.1 Royal Red and Blue", showing royal blue and red squares strokes of paint on a hand-made canvas, and sold at an auction in 2012 for $75 million. Someone may have come up with this idea long before or just as Mark was thinking it – and the only difference was that he took inspiration to act on it. Actions also demonstrate your inspiration, perseverance, and faith in what you believe, and if what you believe in is your success journey and goal, your actions demonstrate that faith. We tend to fail to act on the right things because we're not clear on what it is that we want, what the actions are, or we doubt our ability to set things in motion to accomplish, fearing we will face risks that may seem too high. Action needs to be aligned with your clear purpose to trigger all kinds of brilliant opportunities which in turn will lead you to success. Through the right actions, you allow others to know that you're serious about reaching your goals. Before you know it, other's intentions and goals align with yours. And if they don't align with yours, you will know what to do next. Acting on what needs action will also give you the insight from that experience, for the next actions to take. This includes receiving feedback about improvements. From actions, things that once seemed challenging start to feel easier and your self-confidence in achieving success skyrockets. When you act on the right things, other right things show up and propel you forward and your flow in the right direction accelerates. Goal-setting and planning the right actions to achieve those goals are consequently covered in this phase, while also discovering how to create and seize momentum through spontaneous, inspired actions – those actions that we can often overlook or dismiss.

C – Commit to Model Accountability

Integrity is a word we want to live by, yet often our actions aren't congruent with it. According to the Merriam-Webster dictionary, integrity is the "firm adherence to a code of especially moral or artistic values." Essentially, integrity is about the act of doing the right thing, holding true to what you know is morally right for self and others, regardless of whether it's acknowledged or not, regardless of whether we receive a gain or convenience by the act of doing the right thing. For the sake of integrity, when you make commitments, you hold yourself accountable for what you think, say, and do to hold to that commitment. And because you understand the value of your commitment, it's important to make only those agreements that you intend to keep. Often, too many commitments and agreements are made, and as a result they're not held up. This phase focuses on commitment and accountability to show believing in your solution path and vision of your desired state that it overcomes the challenges and obstacles that come your way. We'll also cover how you can fortify commitment and accountability for yourself and others, to model your clarity and commitment for what it takes to achieve results.

T – Taking Care of Transforming for Success

One of the most important things to include in your leadership strategy is to prioritize self-care. Self-care includes taking care of your mindset so that you can respond effectively to circumstance and events that come your way, with the right mindset and habits that keep you focused on the right things and not get stuck. Many times, we take on too many things, or focus on things that distract us from our focus on the end in mind; and we don't even realize it until we reach a breaking point. Think about what it's costing you not to take care of yourself. What does your quality of work look like when you're over-stressed or stuck in emotions that hold you back from effectively dealing with circumstances and events at work and in your personal life? What triggers your stress level, how, and why? Do you make time to identify them, and how they make you feel or react, so you don't ignore them? Do you know how to release them rather than masking or ignoring them? What are your relationships like at work, in your personal life? Without self-care, or enough self-care, you pay a high cost.

O – Out of The Comfort Zone

I'm not going to lie – it's comfy being in the comfort zone, right? But what if it's getting in the way of you reaching your goal? When you don't push yourself through your comfort zone, that goal of yours could be undermined. In 1908, psychologists Robert M. Yerkes and John D. Dodson did a study on levels of performance and found that in order to maximize performance people needed a state of relative anxiety – what they called "Optimal Anxiety", which is just outside of our comfort zone. They posited that a state of relative comfort creates a steady level of performance, and that we need a state of relative anxiety where stress levels are slightly higher than normal (not too much so that we aren't too stressed to be productive causing performance to drastically drop) in order to maximize performance. You may have experienced this, or just ask anyone who's ever pushed themselves to a higher than norm level or accomplishment – that when you really challenge yourself, you can turn up amazing results, including a high sense of meaningful fulfillment. There are many studies that support this point. It's not to say that your comfort zone is bad – it's neither good nor bad, since it's a natural state. Who wants risk and anxiety (outside of our comfort zone)? But if you know the positive and negative results, understanding what's holding you back can help you decide what's worth it to push through your comfort zone, and if there's something that you can do to feel comfortable with stepping out of that zone to see what's on the other side. In this phase, we'll also review the key negative barriers (e.g., fear, doubt, negative thoughts, emotions) that can cause us to stay in our comfort zone when we should push through it, and key techniques that will support you through setbacks so that you stay on track toward reaching your goals.

R – Relationships That Matter

Remember that song by Barbara Streisand, People Need People? Well, it's true – in work and in life. We live in a relational world where our relationship with everything and people in our lives affects us. It's important to understand the key relationships to keep and the relationships that are toxic, and what to do about that. This includes your relationship with yourself, and how others affect you, thereby impacting your emotions, decisions and behaviour. In this phase, we'll explore the various relationship categories, how we can influence their quality in the context of achieving goals, and why it's important to nurture the right relationships.

***

The FACTOR phases are customized to fit the person. It breaks down each of the elements that successful people who make a difference do on a habitual basis. As you work through this book, you'll see why each step is important, and how you can do it, too, for your leadership goal. If you follow this framework, you will achieve the success you're after, and make a difference in your leadership.

Be Inspired

When you are inspired your focus is endless, clear, and committed to. Imagine the great you that can accomplish with the clarity, know-how, and realization of your desired state: stellar and lasting results of a highly engaged team, a highly engaged you that makes a difference, and who is balanced in all that matters. Making a difference is not just about turning things around, it's about leading yourself and your team to today's victory goal. It's also about ensuring a success path that can be repeated and modelled for sustainability.

I mentioned earlier, my old ways in life took me to a point of involuntary surrender from my "perfect storm" and it was from that surrender I found a need to transform so that I could feel whole again in whatever life presented. Out of that necessity, I found inspiration to uncover the art of my life through purpose. Unbound by the external expectations and label of leadership success, I've found that true leadership is living leadership at an authentic level of perfect imperfections, with all of life's challenges, and amid circumstances that test patterns of thinking, behavior, choices, and actions.

My wish is to share that truth with you in the form of a guiding framework I use for myself and my clients. After all, life is an art. In the words of poet Rainer Maria Rilke, "A work of art is good if it has arisen out of necessity. That is the only way one can judge it."

Now that you know about this framework, take a moment and literally imagine you've reached your desired end state: that you, your team are highly engaged (in the zone of flow), you are known as a great leader that makes a difference, you feel balanced, all within the context of love and joy. Focus on how this makes you feel and write it down, describing how you, your team are (what are you doing, what are they doing, what is the atmosphere like) in this future state. This would be the first building block for building your frame. So just claim your feeling and give it a place of honour in your office. If you can feel it, see it, that's the whisper of truth from your inner leader. Not everyone hears that whisper, though it's there. Take yourself up on that self-anointment as a leader because that's where you start to make a true difference. It is your choice.

Section II

Building the Foundation and Seizing Momentum

Chapter 4:

FRAMING THE FOUNDATION FOR YOUR SUCCESS

"You can be anything you want to be, if only you believe with sufficient conviction and act in accordance with your faith; for whatever the mind can conceive and believe, it can achieve."
– Napoleon Hill, *Think and Grow Rich*

Why Framing Is Important

We all have our own views and opinions, and in business, as you may know, leaders use techniques to influence their organizational views and opinions for increasing effectiveness of aligned focus, engagement and achieving results with their teams. One such technique is called framing, the process of demonstrating a concept, situation, or idea to a clear point that enable others to paint a mental picture of it and gravitate to deciding and acting on it. Generally, framing is the process of communicating a concept, situation, or idea in a manner (visual and in writing) so that others can paint a mental picture of it and decide to either 'get with the 'program', or not. The actions from decisions made are monitored, measured, and

59

managed (in performance management and feedback mechanisms for instance), and further decisions for managing results are made. Essentially, framing is like placing an imaginary frame around an idea or situation to zero in on a certain targeted view or perspective. The effect of framing is what comes out of presenting information in a way that alters or influences yours or someone's decision. Often, this is achieved by using words or visuals that emote someone to feel a certain way about an idea, concept, or situation.

We see this technique used in media, in marketing, in companies when communicating on business changes or new implementations, and even in politics to influence others' views to a particular concept, situation, or idea. In my research on the framing technique, the basic gist for its purpose, is to influence our choices, and more often than not, we fall prey to the framing effect – a cognitive bias in which our brain makes decisions about information, depending on whether the information is presented to us in a positive or negative frame. Born from the development of the prospect theory in the research findings from psychologists and behavioural economic experts Daniel Kahneman and Amos Tversky (Prospect Theory: An Analysis of Decision Under Risk, Econometrica,1979, 47, 263-291), choices can be presented in a way that highlights the positive or negative aspects of the same decision, leading to changes in their relative attractiveness these aspects have on people and their choice to opt for either.

For instance, when one refers to the glass as "half-full", the inference is to be positive and that an adverse situation can be overcome. If one refers to the glass as "half-empty", the inference is that an adverse situation is adverse and that there is little hope to overcome it.

An essential purpose for framing your mind is to improve the focus-to-distraction ratio so that you allow focus on the right things, through the elimination of unnecessary context (variables, factors that don't serve the focus). When the right framing is in place, your ability to focus improves as your attention is narrowed down to the items that need priority focus – no distractions. To kickstart building your mindset foundation, reframe your view of a problem into a solution-oriented way of life and believing that solving something is no more or less a cosmic event as things such as sweeping up the floor after a spill, or showing compassion to an employee who needs constructive feedback, or reflecting on your day's fill of tough decisions, attending to a strategic planning meeting that will discuss lagging results and how to tend to it. I've found that viewing life in this way allows for a healthy detachment of what can constrict true leadership: getting caught up with unnecessary emotional drama that comes with focusing on problems and not solutions. Every focus deserves the same meticulous attention and commitment because they are all opportunities, for better. Every achievement, every failure, is an integral part of life and giving it full and whole attention can make a significant difference in how things work out, for you and thereby, for others. You are a whole person and your life enters the life environments you choose. To view life in this way is to live leadership and your frame of reference comes from your mindset view.

Frame for Focus

Aside from the role-specific talent and technical competencies, successful leaders have a frame of mind that catapults them to exceptional heights in achieving success results, while inspiring others to join them. Such a frame of mind allows for the right focus, the right supporting behaviour, attitude and actions that unleash and make use of the engagement and focus needed to fuel vision and goals achievement. Bill Gates had it with his tenacity to make decisions quickly in a market known for high-change situations. Martin Luther King had it with his focus to turn a dream into a visionary and charismatic leadership for a movement. Winston Churchill had it with his transformational and collaborative public image, notable for his ability to build morale, motivation, and a unified sense of identity. I believe that this frame of mind is the one that defies what, conversely and on average, others default to. This frame of mind I speak of is one in which you use focus as a step to achieve what you want. It is a frame of mind that is guided by the conscious act of deciding what you wish to achieve, deliberately concentrating on and acting on it. It is the frame of mind where "focus" means directing your mental energy and your daily actions (your habits) to be the person you want to be and the focus you want to achieve.

Scientists tell us that we are naturally hardwired for survival and thus initially gravitate to a bias for negativity. Negative experiences stick to our brain so that we can routinely assess risks by making judgements about people and situations for safety measures. To protect us, those negative events that come our way quickly, grab our mind's attention more so than positive ones. For instance, forget the doe and her fawn along the roadside on your way to the cottage. If you don't focus on the winding single lane-road you're driving along at 80 kilometers (50 miles) an hour, you're in the ditch.

Mindset experts tell us that it takes at least three positive thoughts to offset one negative thought. It's no wonder that remaining hopeful and staying the course on a goal seem difficult to maintain when faced with challenges where that bias for negative outcomes bombard us to keep us "safe". When we get stuck in our negative thoughts, we tend to overestimate a situation to conclude impending threats, and underestimate our ability to overcome such threats, thereby underestimating positive possibilities. Without realizing it, we build a view of negative outcomes, such as someone trying to purposely ruin our day by their series of critical questions, when perhaps that person was merely asking questions for better clarification, for collaboration to an even better outcome. The good news is that we can change our frame of mind so that when seeming negativity strikes, we can underestimate negative thoughts of threat and replace them with positive thoughts for possibilities and due diligence actions that serve what we really want to achieve. There is a way, with time-tested strategies that successful leaders use to navigate challenges and obstacles.

Focus and Mindset

With all the distractions in life, it's easy to get focused on things that don't connect to your purpose – your purpose for what you truly want to achieve. In progressive societies, it's become a constant flow of readily available information, some useful and some noisy, entertainment, and insatiable wants for keeping 'in the know' or meeting superficial expectations with our external world's demands and distractions. Right before our eyes and within easy reach, we have access to the constant stream of information, whether we truly need that information or not. We're fed messages from news, blogs, advertisements, articles, television, movies, proposal, and strategy documents setting the parameters for how we are to be, how and what we should want, in our conscious world. We're also fed messages of expectations from colleagues, friends, family, society, anyone we come in regular contact with that show up in our day-to-day lives and expectations of ourselves. Each piece of information enters our mind with one goal: to gain control of our attention and resources, for response. And once our conscious mind accepts each piece of information, it goes into our subconscious mind, shaping our way of thinking and behaving.

Knowing what information is deemed as a distraction and what is important have become more difficult for many of us to discern, as we habitually sift through and react to the myriad of messages and information coming from everywhere. As a result, many of us live our lives distracted by unconscious habits that keep us in that hamster wheel of crossing off a long list of unqualified "to-do's" and "have-to's", limiting our ability to focus, create and accomplish anything meaningful. And we may even find ourselves relating with others out of obligation, or a routine of "doing", so much so that we've lost clear purpose for why, simply for – you guessed, it – distracting us. When we find ourselves on this wheel, responsibility wanes for living a life of attentive, intentional living – keeping us in a life of distraction, rather than true meaning. It's all too easy to find ourselves at the mercy of our distractions. You may know it well as you recall the acceptable words you exchange with others like, "I don't have enough time", or "I wish I had more time, but..."

Make sure you're certain about what you need to focus on and what distractions to keep away from. It's like what movie producer Martin Scorsese says, "Cinema is a matter of what's in the frame, and what's out." Or, like what an architect plans for his dream bungalow home with a deck overlooking a lake. A frame for a high-rise building wouldn't be constructed. Framing for the right focus is about the choices you make, what you want to focus on achieving at your desired end state, what actions you will take and how you respond to every situation to get there. Framing for right focus, then, is a preliminary step to help minimize distractions that get in the way of achieving goals. It's about framing your mind, making sure you have the right mindset as your foundation, so that you're clear on what it is you do want and what goals and actions it takes, to be ready for handling all the variables and distractions that will inevitably come your way when striving to achieve, perform, relate. Your frame of mind is your mindset which is what supports you in what you determine are distractions, opportunities, and what the necessary elements are for responding to what's happening in your life. Your mindset – the distinguishable and patterned mental attitude that determines how you'll interpret and respond to situations – is what supports your individual thoughts, decision-making, capability, and capacity for what you act on, and how you act in response to any of these environments that are operating in your life. It is the support-base for your outcomes in these environments. Your thoughts completely control your destiny for every aspect of your life because it's from your thoughts where actions and outcomes result.

From a cause and effect perspective, your thoughts are the cause of your results, both personal and professional. Creating the right mindset allows for creating thoughts that align with your goal, and replacing thoughts, beliefs and behaviours that don't.

Understanding Where You Fall in The Mindset Continuum

Your mindset is where you hold your beliefs about yourself and the how the world around you fits into and influences those beliefs. An informative and easy-to-read book to learn more about mindsets is Carol S. Dweck's book, Mindset: The New Psychology of Success. In it, she highlights two types of opposing mindsets: the fixed mindset and the growth mindset. Those with a fixed mindset hold the belief that traits, talents, and intelligence are fixed and cannot be changed. Carol posits that those with a fixed mindset "worry about their traits [and talents] and how adequate they are" and are usually driven by having "to prove something to themselves and others." While in comparison, those with a growth mindset view their traits and talents as something that can be developed and grown through effort, commitment, and accountability. Those with a growth mindset thrive on learning, developing, growing, and they view their potential as limitless. She further demonstrates in her research findings that each of these mindsets are on the opposite ends of a continuum – which highlights that somewhere along this continuum, is where each of our mindset falls. She reports in The Atlantic article "How Praise Became a Consolation Prize" (December 16, 2016), "Nobody has a growth mindset in everything all the time. Everyone is a mixture of fixed and growth mindsets. You could have a predominant growth mindset in an area but there can still be things that trigger you into a fixed mindset trait." These triggers surface beliefs and behaviours from past negative experiences that have not been fully dealt with and resolved at the conscious level such as childhood traumas of abuse or feelings of fear and failure. So which end of the continuum serves us best for achieving success, particularly for the sake of progression or achieving desired results? I believe the right end of the continuum is along the growth mindset. Developing a growth mindset is crucial to succeed in anything – it's the most important component of your journey's foundation to achieving success. When I decided to switch my career in 2005 from employment to owning my own consulting and coaching business,

I knew that there was a way for me. I held faith to my purpose, tested, optimized, and seized momentum for getting out there to learn, adjust, and expand my network for opportunities – and I knew it would pay off eventually. I had a gut-feeling of it – it did pay off, and it's ongoing. I was on the right path, because I set a mindset to align with my ongoing path for what I progressively wanted, not what I didn't want.

When building the right mindset, it's like building a home: your blue print is created by your clear vision for what makes a house feel like home to you (your end in mind) and you hold to that vision with your mindset as the foundation. When I refer to "feel", I mean really feel the feelings from a place of love, connection and joy for that vision. Picture yourself in that beautiful kitchen, that family room with the joyful memories you'll create with your loved ones if that is your vision. Your vision could be that you and your team have achieved the results with stellar performance where everyone is productive, highly engaged. Within the mindset are guiding elements needed to form the right thoughts, beliefs, behaviour/attitude, decisions, actions, and habits to effectively attract the positive emotions and feelings (and even resources) that support you for what it takes to create the reality of your vision. By this, you will be able to respond effectively to those opportunities, obstacles and challenges that will come along the way, not stay in your current state that does not serve your focus.

Here are some of the key focus areas, at a minimum for setting the right mindset:

Critical Reflection for Current State Clarification

Critical reflection is more than just "thinking about" something. It is a way of evaluating yourself and situations in a rigorous way – helping you to carefully consider what is good and what could be improved. It is vital to make mindset change positive and productive. It involves trying to make sense of what happened to create your current state and it means looking for answers about the personal issues that have arisen, and which are patterns from past experiences. Critical reflection is a genuine deep search from within for what's led to the current state – an examination of cause and effect relationships, resulting responsive emotions, behavioural patterns and actions that have been embedded as habits. When critical self-reflection occurs, it enables the ability to move on from seeking to blame and relinquish responsibility for outcomes.

Discovery and Exploration of Options for Future State Clarification

This is the part of transformation when you become aware of the possibility for changing your reality through self-empowerment, from a vision that incorporates what you have realized about your core passions, joys, values, needs. This awareness empowers you to consider alternative and solutions-oriented options for a better future state utilizing the awareness of your true purpose, your abilities and power that may have been untried in the past. Appreciative inquiry, visualization and affirmation tools and techniques are typically used to fortify the positive mental images for what a better future the person envisions. These tools also help to unfold the right positive emotions and feelings (joy, excitement, love) to discover the right actions and habits that serve the decided future state vision.

Shift Your Beliefs for Success

When you shift your beliefs for success' realization, it is all about the realization that certain things are permissible, achievable and even good. For instance, Wendy, a VP client of mine realized for the first time that it was okay for her to refuse to perform tasks that were not her responsibility; rather, they were her colleague's and even her direct leader's. This strikes at the belief that a nice person and a good co-worker or direct report should please people – a belief she once had, until she realized through her overload of work and commitments, that such a belief was not serving her in being at her best in work and home life.

Resolution and Planning

Once learning, reflection, and awareness of self-image and world-view are in place, the realization of your desired future state becomes imminent along with the forming of plans to build and practice through actions and new habits.

Considering the above, challenges will come up, testing your current thinking, and consequently, impacting your decisions, actions, and outcomes. These challenges are a result of the systems and frameworks that exist in the organization, in your relationships, and in your personal life, and how your mindset has been shaped from past experiences. What if in that gap between where you are (highly disengaged team and the results you need them to align to in achieving) and where you want to be/or what you want to achieve (high engagement that lasts for meeting results and continues on for the next results target), your thinking misguides your decision-making and the actions needed to address the gap to getting there? What if you do not have a clear picture of what your current state is really all about? What if you're incomplete with your picture of what your future desired state is? What if you think that you're not a very good leader today but want to be – as if today you're overwhelmed and not feeling capable of solving this? What if your team members are tired and disengaged because they feel the same and you have an opportunity to make a difference for them?

Know What Affects You

In the previous chapter, I covered a bit about getting from point A (current state) to point B (desired end state), and the in-between elements causing the gap between the points. What's in the gap between the two is a revelation to what your priority focus needs to include, to ensure you address what's in the gap to get to your desired end state. In this gap are all the things that come up which may hinder you from getting to the state you want. Determining what these things are, requires you to be aware of and fully in tune with the external variables and factors, as well as, and most importantly, the inner variables and factors, from within you. This inner view requires inner work, namely, mindset work – a shift in mindset to allow for healthy reflection and introspection, processing and releasing of negative thoughts, behaviours, feelings from emotions so that your responsive actions do not hinder you, but rather serve you to getting what you want. It's called inner "work" because it takes work and regular commitment and effort.

Systems and Frameworks at Play

In a later section, I cover the importance of relationships and how keeping to the right relationships is critical for the right mindset. For now, knowing what affects you personally, from a systems standpoint is an important and fundamental relationship concept to understand, so that you're aware of what really hits your internal "plate" at source – those systems from the environment you show up in, which affect your thinking, decisions, behaviour, and actions.

In this relational world we live in, an individual's sense of identity is affected by the environment we choose to be in – environments such as family, social relationships, community, society, and work. Each environment has their own principles, disciplines, processes to react, respond to, sustain – principles, disciplines and processes that make up a system/framework. When you choose to operate in these environments, you must adapt. These systems/frameworks are interconnected because they're attached to the whole you – you experience them as interconnected environments in your life and relationships. As a result, when you choose to relate in these environments, they call upon you (your mindset) to respond. Your mindset conditions itself to these environments. In the analogy of house-building, then, your entire house is made up of all this, and what you frame as your mindset foundation, is what supports your house.

In the business/career world, every person in an organization is bound by systems and frameworks (principles, disciplines, processes, rules) that impose a response by the individual, because the organization must ensure its existence and progress are safeguarded through alignment of everyone's performance. For instance, job roles must be performed, decisions and approvals must be made, relationships must be managed, risk management guidelines must be fulfilled, and business results must be achieved. This general organizational system framework has sub-frameworks too (e.g., frameworks that come from Human Resources programs or "people programs" that guide performance and motivate employee engagement; frameworks for service delivery, financial regulatory, legal requirements, for decision and authority levels, and so forth). Now add to this, an individual's personal system/frameworks from other aspects of their life – family, social, societal, and personal relationships. Whether one knows it or not, these exist and show up simultaneous to those organizational system/frameworks. Many leaders spend more time with measuring an individual's work performance and connection requirements to the organization's system/frameworks, that easily forgotten is the individual's personal internal system/frameworks at play also – their personal life principles, disciplines, processes affecting their beliefs, emotional attachments, relationships, decisions, and responsive actions. The personal frame of reference is also affected by your past experiences that have conditioned your mindset (thoughts, beliefs and resulting emotional capacity) to respond to and handle current circumstances and situations.

Employee engagement measures the level of connection an employee has, based on selected elements that drive engagement from within the organization's system/frameworks – those elements that, according to best practice, are highly correlated with the employee's level of connection with the organization and therefore, alignment for desired performance levels. These elements include the company's vision/mission/purpose/values, leadership, performance evaluation, experience of workplace culture, work and life balance, compensation and benefits, communication, relationship with manager, provision of tools and equipment to do job effectively, personal accomplishment on the job, growth opportunities, and a clear line of sight that everyone is able to describe how their job links to company's long-term objectives). Think about this as a leader and how this affects your team members also. What's missing in these engagement scores is the full picture of other elements influencing the individual (you or your team members).

You are a whole being, made up of a multitude of roles and levels of performance that call upon you from more than one system/framework. If these systems/frameworks are happening simultaneously, that employee engagement scores report you have in your hands only tells you one side of the whole picture to issues you may be facing.

You may recall the analogy I used in an earlier chapter about the perfect storm. In the context of all these frameworks at play, as a leader then, ask yourself if a perfect storm could occur for you, for your team members, when all these frameworks are at play and converge, collide. When left unattended or not prioritized, effects experienced in any one of these frameworks could merge with another, causing dilemmas – dilemmas for you as the individual leader, and thus for your team and for the organization. A collision in contradiction to any one of the principles, disciplines, and processes inherent within those systems/frameworks, can cause havoc for the individual, leading to experience a disconnect from feeling whole. Choices made with inevitable dilemmas also inherent in any one or all of these frameworks could be based on a mindset that doesn't allow for effective decision making and the right resulting actions to fix your situation on a sustainable basis. Imagine also if this could happen to you, what a ripple effect it could be, and multiply that effect by the number of individuals on your team.

As a leader, striving to make a difference with turning things around for you and your team's engagement and alignment to results achievement requires attention to a misconception that may be getting in the way of resolving the right issue – the misconception that there is a solution to seek out from others when it comes to engagement. Possible solutions are already within your reach, by changing your perspective, and then modeling that for others to do same.

The 101 of Mindset

The mind is unique to each of us, created from relationships that influence our personal sense of and need for self-identity. Our thoughts, feelings, perceptions, memories, beliefs, attitudes, and regulatory patterns are unique. Neuroscience tells that there is this Reticular Activation System (RAS) in our brain, the gatekeeper of information from external places that is filtered into our conscious mind (a network of nerve pathways in the brainstem connecting the spinal cord, cerebrum, and cerebellum, and mediating the overall level of our consciousness). This RAS distinguishes what's relevant and what's not relevant info for us. The RAS is a small part of the brain (apparently the size of a pencil) but it is important for attention, goal-achievement, and keeping us alive. All our senses (except smell) are apparently directly related to this bundle of neurons. The RAS is a filter – like a security guard – working for our brain to make sure our brain doesn't have to deal with more info that it can handle. Thus, the RAS plays a big role in the sensory info we perceive daily. What's further intriguing is that our senses (sight, touch, hearing, taste) receive tons of information that gets processed in the conscious part of our mind, the part of our mind that makes the decision for our reaction. While our conscious mind has limited information processing capacity (basically meaning it has short-term memory of the information it receives) its power is that it's the part of our brain that thinks and reasons (for our everyday decisions), accepts or rejects any idea or thought – and we can actually influence what information we want it to decide. The other part of our mind, the subconscious, has an incredible information processing capacity, with no ability to reject ideas and thoughts, and receives whatever information our conscious mind accepts so that a decisive reaction can take place. Always operating to respond in the present, it stores and draws from past learning, experiences, and memories from its receipt of conscious thoughts, forming our beliefs, attitudes, values, self-image, and habits in response to events. Studies tell us that we take in anywhere from about 50,000 to 75,000 thoughts a day and about 35-48 thoughts per second. So, this RAS, your conscious and subconscious mind, are critical for filtering our thought retention and processing for the rest of our physiology to respond. Unfortunately, many have conditioned their mindset to a programming that Fortunately, we can condition our mindset at any given moment – when we consciously decide so.

The Five Factors to Condition the Right Mindset

The right mindset foundation for harnessing success, requires at least five foundational factors that go into the right conditioning to allow for success realization. These five factors, once applied and nurtured, can help guide your mindset frame for your transformative process to change your thoughts and beliefs to a positive behavioural pattern that aligns with your habits that serve your goal to be a leader that makes a difference.

- Factor of Awareness – being aware of key elements that influence the right mindset;
- Factor of Responding with response-ability – taking full responsibility for your responses to influence outcomes from circumstances you experience;
- Factor of Having a clarity of purpose – being clear on your purpose;
- Factor of Having a clarity for what is wanted – being clear on what it is you want; and
- Factor of creating a frequency to attract what you want, not on what you don't want – how your thoughts and feelings attract your outcomes.

Important to note is that because each person is unique, the consideration and the application of these factors must be customized to everyone's personal transformative needs. It's helpful to work with a coach through this personalization to provide objectivity and accountability for support in the transformative process.

Awareness

Awareness is the ability to gain knowledge or perception of a situation or fact, and foundational to guiding what action to take. You're practicing awareness right now just by reading this book. I have found that awareness that serves true purpose is the single most essential ingredient for developing the right mindset for achieving progress, success in environments requiring a level of optimal performance. It allows you to be proactive to influence things in your life through your thoughts, beliefs, and habits. Many, however, are aware of only those things that distract from what should be focused on to achieve what is truly wanted. Awareness impacts your thoughts which determine your way of thinking, and what you do with that thinking to influence your behaviuor.

As mentioned earlier, thinking is what shapes your beliefs and how you respond to the variables in your life, thereby shaping your actions (habits) and outcomes. The key is to harness the kind of awareness that guides you for what to do with what you become aware of. To become aware in this way, determine what distracts you in your head and how to get you back on track to achieving your performance goals as a whole person, because it serves a purpose for your vision, not for keeping you stuck in your emotions that shape actions (habits) that are contrary to moving you forward. Becoming aware of what distracts you may include the discovery of past traumas that may require deep processing with the guiding help of experts such as a therapist or a coach. Seeking and putting in place such supports are important.

Awareness can provide insight into where you're progressing and where you're stuck. If you're aware, then you'll know what you need to do and the direction you need to go to make improvements toward success for what you want. Awareness also makes you seek out more insightful information about what beliefs are holding you back, and how to change them, from what beliefs you should have that serve your purpose. When you're aware, you've opened yourself to the essential information needed for your action-based thinking that sticks to success – the awareness of what you need to do to move forward.

Remember that as a leader, you've anointed yourself into a role that's largely outward looking – meaning that much of your efforts are focused on external factors such as steering the organization's vision, strategy, strategic articulation through your team members, influencing others, inspiring, guiding, and evaluating others' performance levels except your own. This means that what is not usually accounted for is the self-evaluative piece, from within. When you include a focus on your inner self, you evaluate your own true drivers for performance, based on setting the right mindset for success: how you perceive the world around you, how you perceive yourself in the world, how you feel you need to be perceived by others. Maybe you present yourself to others as this inspired, positive, energetic, and motivating leader to your team and colleagues, but deep down you know or feel it's all a farce, that really you feel like a fake or could be doing more or something different, something more aligned to your true purpose. Maybe you've got your own personal performance struggles and you try to keep things together for everyone else's sake. Maybe you could be changing your own habits so that you can model what it is that inspires others or shows them the way to get out of dragging their heels or being sick and tired of the same unengaging things that caused them to drag their heels in the first place. What happens when your leadership lens for your outward view and goals are skewed, clouded or grimy? Would you be able to clearly inspire, guide, and evaluate the performance of your team, leading them to victory? It's not that you don't want to keep connected with the inward, but when you're so focused on the outward, looking inward can be a challenge because your compass is not clear. And when this happens, you create a distorted outcome that shows your disengagement, or causes disengagement. For instance, imagine the always-on

VP who eventually suffers burn out; or the leader who is never seen by the team; or the micromanager who hovers rather than delegates; or the control-obsessed manager who only delegates meaningless tasks leaving the team's talent underutilized; or the leader who believes in status quo and anything the team says or does outside of their direction is always wrong or dismissed. These management scenarios do not reflect the inward self-evaluation that's needed and because of this, they are not aware of (though should be) of important factors and considerations, nor do they care about how their behaviour may adversely impact the team and thus, the organization. Self-awareness, introspection, and self-actualization go a long way toward achieving personal growth that significantly improves leadership for engaging self and others.

Here are some of the preliminary awareness questions I ask my clients to gauge their mindset:

- Who do you believe you are? And why?
- What areas in your life require you to play a role and produce results for others? What are those roles?
- Are you aware of what's around you? What are they? How do those people, things/circumstances affect you? How do you affect those people, things/circumstances?
- Do you believe you're fully aware of what you need to be aware of?
- What challenges are you facing right now? How do these challenges make you feel?
- What do you want your life to be like without those challenges?
- What do you believe is your part in resolving those challenges?

Self-Awareness

Self-awareness is important in every aspect of life. It's essential when dealing with relationships, and as a leader, it's key for self-engagement before you can engage your team. If you're aware of the things you say and do, you'll be able to recognize when your actions send the wrong signal to your team, causing disengagement, tiredness, or distraction from the results you want yourself and your team to focus on. This may sound straightforward, but it takes some people years before they understand what this concept means, and how to apply it to their life. It's an ongoing process, really, and it takes regular practice before it can move from thoughts, to beliefs, to becoming a habit. Techniques such as meditation can help guide and strengthen self-awareness.

What Does It Mean to Be Self-Aware?

Self-awareness is when you have a solid understanding about who you are, what triggers you and how you relate to the world (through your relationships, whether at work or in personal life). This solid understanding comes from being mentally and emotionally present in your situations and understanding how those situations affect you, how you respond, and how your actions affect you and others. It also means that you're clued into to what you really enjoy and dislike. According to some psychologists, we have two types of self-awareness: public self-awareness and private self-awareness. The public self-awareness surfaces when we are aware of how we appear to others such as in the case when we're presenting to a group. This type of awareness tends to make us comply or be astute to social norms and cues, and affects how we tend to behave so that we can influence how we are perceived by society and the relationships we have in society. Anxiety, stress, and worry from how others view or evaluate us can be as a result of our public self-awareness. The private self-awareness surfaces when we become aware of some aspects of ourselves in a private way. For example, you feel depressed, heavyhearted from sad news you've just heard. In another example, you could be feeling butterflies in your stomach just before you go on stage for your speech or presentation; or that pit in your stomach just before your termination notice to an employee; or feeling your stomach tighten when you realize you forgot to prepare for an important meeting requiring your update. I guide my clients through self-reflection exercises to explore awareness and self-awareness in scenarios like these. I have them make a list of how they think their public self-awareness surfaces in their work and personal life. Try it. Do the same for your private self-awareness. See for yourself what comes up. And if this boggles you pre or during this exercise, consider a coach to help you. It'll do you wonders.

Many things in life trigger emotions that affect our thoughts, good or bad, and can often cloud self-awareness (maybe even shut it down). Take our childhood upbringing for instance. As kids we were taught to behave in a certain way, which almost always influences how we view and approach things in our adult life. For example, "do what you're told" can be carried into our adult life believing that it is wrong to question status quo. Another example is how media portrays what success or beauty should look like. Magazines, ads, etc., equate success with being a millionaire-plus, or equate beauty with made-up, thin, and ageless looking men and woman. We see the same kind of thing in an organization, where we learn what's acceptable, the rules around what we're supposed to do, how many hours we must work, how to look 'busy' for status or the almighty dollar. To start waking up your self-awareness, ask yourself if this rings true to you. What, from your past or present triggers you that may be distracting your focus for moving forward in the present with true purpose. Gauge it from how it makes you feel emotionally, mentally, physically, intellectually, morally. Then, see if you feel a sense of lack, or passion that's not being met from how you really want to behave for more of the true you to come out. Some signs limited self-awareness include:

- Feeling as though everyone else is always to blame for things that are happening to you
- Complaining about your lot in life
- Complaining and judging others
- Feeling overwhelmed by your schedule
- Feeling like you don't have enough time

- A craving for more balance
- Feeling guilty or the need to have to please people
- Constantly apologizing or not being able to accept apologies
- Over-apologizing
- Feeling apathy
- Obsessing on an emotion, or an event that occurred
- Over-thinking

These signs are examples of the kind of reflection you may need to become more self-aware. These signs are also examples of sources for why negative outcomes keep showing up in your life.

You're not alone in this. Many go through this, including leaders who have successfully gained their leadership career. It's a human, natural built-in self-preservation instinct to hold back from self-awareness, to experience raw emotions from events or situations that we become aware of. The good news is that becoming more self-aware is a continual process that zeros in on what you will want to do with what you notice. The more self-aware you are, the more clarity you will find, the more you will know, the better you can reprogram your emotional response and attachment to situations and events that come your way, to serve your true purpose.

Introspection

Introspection is the process of consciously looking at what you have become self-aware of, observing, and determining the way you think, feel, believe, and behave from that self-awareness. It allows you to make use of your self-awareness for deciding what changes and improvements you need to make with your behaviour for what you want out of your life. Introspection can bring to the surface some things about you that you may not have previously been aware of. For some, this can be an emotionally-charging experience. I recommend you prepare for this by getting a coach to help you through this process (for some, it may also be appropriate to seek therapy counseling).

When I work with my clients, I have them start the framing process by assessing their level of self-awareness – identifying and describing their key life environments in their current state: work, home, relationships. This helps to identify at what initial stage of awareness they may be and what they need to focus on. Almost always, I find many are at the initial stage of holding tight to their view that they don't have enough time.

Tips to Make Time for Your Growth in Awareness

The following tactics are helpful for finding the time for personal growth and practicing self-awareness:

Set a healthy pace for performance, with productivity: It's true that life can move quickly, and in the workplace, there can be so much expected from us to do within tight timelines. With technology becoming more and more advanced, there are efficiency measures and practices that are available that can be leveraged to enable healthy pace with high productivity. As a leader, start with your own level of pace and productivity. Do an audit of what keeps you busy, calibrate and look for ways to improve your time management by prioritizing based on core targets, strengths and talents (core genius). Knowing what activities to delete, defer/delay, or delegate can help significantly. Delegation can help leverage and enable your team's core genius, while at the same time allowing you to keep to your core genius and promote a healthy pace within your own schedule of to-do's. As Stephen Covey reminds us in *7 Habits of Highly Effective People*, put first things first (Habit #3) and synergize (Habit #6).

Be mindful of overstimulation: When we are overstimulated, the time it takes to process incoming thoughts becomes too much for us to balance which results in not being able to retain the information we are trying to process. Organize the information coming in that's needed and prioritize what needs tending to.

Commit to personal growth: through self-awareness (know yourself), continuous learning, passion, making sure you have personal time to focus on your personal growth, seek and embrace feedback, seek opportunities to leverage your core strengths and talents.

Practice meditation: Meditation is an excellent means for opening up to self-awareness and self-observation, and there are many excellent guiding sources for meditation out there. Just Google it, you'll see. There are forms of meditation purely for awareness, for self-observation, anxiety, letting go of negative emotions, tuning into your body, relaxation. You may already have some sources you're using to help you. Some of my favourite sources come from MindValley, Jack Canfield, Deepak Chopra, and Robin Sharma. Yoga and tai-chi are also excellent practices to blend into your meditation practice. Another excellent self-awareness technique I share with my clients is Emotional Freedom Technique (EFT, Tapping) which not only helps with awareness, but also helps with processing what you discover about yourself that may cause emotional-based symptoms such as anxiety and body ailments. If you have a coach, they will likely have recommendations too.

Response-Ability

Through my certification to train clients on Jack Canfield's the Success Principles™, there are about 67 principles/habits for success which I integrate for guiding others in their transformation journey. Taking full responsibility for yourself is one of the fundamental habits which forms the basis for all the other principles. Would you believe me if I told you that you are creating your experiences, your success, the quality of your relationships and your health, by your thoughts, the beliefs you focus on and the emotions they create for you; and that you have total control over these? Believe it. Beliefs are no more than thoughts you've thought about over and over and embedded in your mind as true. Therefore, you act out from those thoughts.

A characteristic of a successful leader is being responsible for and demonstrating those habits that show and model responsibility, from the inside-out. Having the ability to take full responsibility for anything that comes your way is critical for engagement and takes the right mindset.

Choose your mindset that serves your true purpose and passion. If you start the week telling yourself that it is going to be awful, any task or change will likely add to you feeling more awful. Instead, start with a mindset that supports you and builds confidence. Tell yourself, "there is a lot to do but I can do it and do it well." By adjusting your mindset, you can respond more proactively and be more productive.

As I've come to learn, taking full responsibility means taking yourself and helping others to take themselves out of the blaming/complaining game. It is often too easy to fall into the trap of blaming others for how we feel and for what happens to us. Blaming abolishes your ability to take full responsibility for what you do with situations that happen inevitably in your life. When you blame, you really can't do anything with the situation because you're focused on something that has already happened and you can't undo it from happening – that's the past, so blaming is futile. When you catch yourself blaming a situation and others, try to be aware that it isn't useful. Take it as a signal to evaluate yourself and to do something more useful. When we blame, we judge others, because it's our internal stuff we have to clean out.

Similarly, complaining is not very useful, except as a signal for more introspection. When we complain, we have a reference point for something better than what we are facing at the time, but we don't want to take the risk of changing how it shows up in our life. For instance, if you complain about someone not pulling their weight on a task at work, and you're taking on more as a result, maybe you're complaining because you want less work to worry about, but you aren't prepared to make that happen through options like delegating. Perhaps this is the case because you don't want to take risk of having them say no for fear of making them more disengaged. Or perhaps, you have issues of trust. When you complain, be aware that you can do something about it, and introspect on why you're complaining, what the risks are that you are not prepared to take to do something about what you're complaining about. Look at it this way, do you complain about gravity? No. Why? Because you accept that there is no alternative, so you go about your life, with gravity, accordingly. Here's the thing, the only thing you can do something about is to respond to a situation effectively and know that the only thing you can influence are your thoughts, beliefs, and the mental images you have in response to the situation that has happened.

Choose to take full responsibility by focusing on your response to the situation/event, and what you want the desired outcome to be so that it best serves you in the future. Drawing from my training of Canfield's success principles, I demonstrate and clarify this concept extensively with clients – the concept of a life approach where you are curious about what you could do, could fix, could be more aware of, to resolve a situation, by pulling your future desired outcome into your present moment so that it shapes your response and next action steps. Future desired outcome, by the way, is not about a reactive response – a reactive response usually produces an emotionally-charged response that wreaks with blame or complain, that gets stuck in the past. What you want is a proactive response for the ideal future and your ideal future which includes mitigating negativity that causes you to operate reactively, in the present moment – that moment when you react to the situation. I have learned that there are three responses that are the only things you have control over which help you to pull the future into to your present: your thoughts and beliefs (e.g., self-talk, conscious, and sub-conscious); your behaviour (including what you say and how you say it); and your visual imagery (including your visualization of your desired future state).

Another important tidbit about taking full responsibility is that it increases your self-esteem and confidence level from knowing and believing you can influence your outcomes because you look for solutions within your inner capability and create them for the outcomes you want. You take the position one cannot rewind time, that you are responsible for your responses in the now, and you feel empowered to do so. When you can do this for yourself through regular practice, you can model it to your team, enabling empowerment which is key to engagement. By doing so, you and others progress in the right direction – forward.

Something I guide my clients on is personal journaling, which helps them record their thoughts based on a narrowed focus on what can serve them in their goals. In one exercise, I get them to make an initial list of what areas they feel they might be able to take more responsibility in their key areas of life (work, personal, relationships, financial, body/ health, leisure/recreation, and community/global contribution), and then we revisit it in our subsequent coaching sessions and what they feel they need to focus on. This helps in at least two ways: to zero in on what matters most in each key are; and to start flexing on thinking with the headspace of taking full responsibility through their influence of response to an event (for the sake of desired future outcome) versus influencing the event that already happened.

Another area of focus I guide my clients on is helping them to shift their attitude toward taking full responsibility for situations that have happened and that they have to deal with. Knowing what to take full responsibility for is uncovered in self-awareness. I use a series of tools and techniques which help to reinforce that it takes practice to learn a new habit. Regularly applying a tool or technique takes practice and more practice until it becomes a habit. For instance, to increase awareness and grow knowledge, see about obtaining ideas from external information that serves your focus, e.g., books, colleagues who can help, social media on target topics, a good personal coach. Practice this daily until it sticks as a habit. Experts tell us that it takes a minimum of thirty days of regular practice for a habit to start forming.

To get started with practicing right habits, you must know what you are addressing. Here are some exercises and coaching guidance I cover with clients for getting to know themselves (and for me getting to know them):

- What does success mean to you and is it aligned with your awareness of your true purpose and passion, core genius and skills?
- What are your successes to date, personally and professionally and what do you do to celebrate these success and leverage for future successes?
- What feelings come up when you feel successful? What approaches did you take to get you to those successes?
- Are you aware of natural laws in life that can help you to achieve what you want in your life? How do you feel about this as a possibility for you in your success path? Note: to learn more about natural laws, check out Deepak Chopra's The Seven Spiritual Laws of Success where he covers pure potentiality, giving, cause and effect, least effort, intention and desire, detachment, purpose in life.
- Practice and act from unusual clarity of focus and purpose. Do you know what this is and do you want to know more? How clear are you about your focus? Do you focus on the past, the present or the future, and to what extent in each? Do you know what your purpose and passion in life is and if so, what are they?
- Justify your actions. What are your day-to-day habits? What motivates you to act? What causes you to not act and why?
- Seek clarity. What does clarity mean to you? What do you feel you're clear on in your life and what you're not clear on? Who do you seek clarity from?
- Kill perfectionism. What does this mean to you? What areas in your life have you felt you are being a perfectionist in if at all?
- Be open to feedback. What does feedback mean to you? Who gives you feedback now and on what? How do you feel about the feedback you're receiving today and what further feedback do you feel you still need? Why?
- Acknowledge that every 'first time' will be difficult. List your 'first time' experiences that you feel were difficult for you,

describing why, how it made you feel, and the outcomes to those experiences.

- Be aware of and tackle your mental and emotional blocks. What does this mean to you and what comes up for you in this?
- Be patient and practice as a student. What does this mean to you and how might it apply to you?
- Don't expect comfort. What makes you feel comfortable and how does it make you feel? List three key experiences you've had where you've not been comfortable, how each made you feel, and the outcomes to them.

Clarity of Purpose

A key success habit of great leaders is their distinctive clarity of purpose and vision, producing results, emulating the right habits, and inspiring from this place of clarity. For some organizations, an organizational vision, purpose/mission, and values are clearly stated, which may or may not have included employee involvement. If employees were effectively involved in the shaping of it, it's considered as best practice and a good start for engagement. A deeper level engagement opportunity is providing time for leaders and team members to express their individual personal purpose and vision, so that they can see how it aligns with the organization's. Once you allow time for yourself to gain clarity of your own purpose (achieved through uncovering your passion, joys, strengths and needs), you can have your team go through a similar process and reinforce the value of committing to this through your one-on-one coaching. Human Resources may also be able to help within their employee relations role. Clarity of purpose is about the work that clarifies one's personal "why" in all they do and for what life purpose.

Knowing your "why" and true purpose unleashes your source for passion, your true sense of self. That special amazing "something" that makes you want to do what you do, that makes you go the extra mile. Passion is that hard-to-put-a-finger-on-it mojo that puts you in your state or zone of creative flow for producing and performing within your core natural talent and purpose. Passion defines your purpose in life and when uncovered and nurtured daily, your level of engagement and productivity is limitless. Doing what you do best gives you energy, keeps you engaged and gives you a sense of who you are, a sense for balance with use of your time.

Tips to Try for Yourself, and Engage Others to Do Same

In the workplace, look for ways you can allow for your team to find purpose and passion and how it fits in what they do at work. This can create a bond amongst you and the organization. Keeping personal passion and purpose alive is the respective individual's responsibility. Yet, organizations can help enable them to do so when in the workplace, while at the same time being able to get real-time calibration for alignment with the organization's performance needs. Some ways you can do this is by leveraging your regular team or one-on-one meetings to allow for two-way discussion and exercises for your team members to participate in, which helps them to discover their passions and purpose, how these can be woven into the organization's mission, vision, and values, supporting strategies, their own jobs, role, and accountability clarity in the organization.

Balancing the level of importance and alignment between a person's passion and purpose with the organization's mission, vision, and values requires your leadership and your strategy for balancing through daily activities, meetings, and coaching sessions. Finding passion and keeping it alive requires self-awareness. If you want to discover your purpose, you need to understand your own passion, joys, and values. We are faced with so much "wanting" and "having" that we tend to lose sight of what our true purpose is, for what's truly important to achieve in the first place. At some level, most of us know that "more" and "faster" are promissory notes that lay claim on our time and effort, to our families, to our energy, and to our hearts. While there is no single answer to the question "How much is enough?", having a clarity of true purpose – your true sense of self – helps to guide how you manage your thoughts, beliefs, and actions which serve that true purpose.

For my clients, I use psychometric assessment tools to maintain a level of objectivity when working with them through their process of discovering their passions (joys, values, strengths, needs) and how these significantly impact and clarify their "why" (purpose). There are many psychometric tools available that test various traits such as personality, intelligence, attitude, and beliefs, and values. These traits are important characteristics that provide the individual with guiding insight into what truly drives them at core. Once discovered, a following technique is reviewing these passions to discover how these are showing up in one's life and choices – the jobs/roles they take on in the business world over the course of their career, their patterned approach with their social relations, hobbies, volunteer work, and so forth. Discovering common themes across their life experiences helps to further clarify "why" they do the things they do – which is either serving true passion and purpose, or not.

Clarity of What You Want

Another key success habit of successful leaders is finding clarity for what they want. They are so clear about what they want, that they are not only specific about it, but they are specific in their focus for what's involved and what actions they commit to. Often, people aren't clear on what it is they want. They focus on what they don't want rather than focusing on what they do want. They're easily distracted by their emotions, or tasks that don't achieve much else than what they don't want. When working with clients, I've either asked the question or the topic comes up to explore, "Is your life in balance?" From line-staff workers, to senior management, and executives, nearly everyone's response points to the answer – the want to find a way to keep doing what they're doing at work while still being able to tuck their kid in at night, or spend time with their friends, or just take a breather. Being clear on what you want is key to keeping your frame of focus (and supportive mindset). From that focus, you will be able to keep your thoughts, beliefs, and actions on what it will take and what you are prepared to do.

Visualization – the process of forming a mental image of something – is a great way to help accelerate achieving something because it enables you to have a clear picture (vision) of what you want. It does this in at least three profound ways. First, it activates our conscious mind's ability to hold focus on what you are visualizing, thereby enabling your subconscious mind's ability to retain mental images of something and influences our beliefs (repetitive thoughts) to align with that mental image. Secondly, it enables our brain to notice available resources that we may not have realized was available to us through our brain's Reticular Activating System (RAS). According to neuroscience, this plays a significant role in our cognitive functions related to awareness and other important functions like sleep and waking, behavioural motivation, our heart beating, and breathing. Last, but not least, visualization helps to draw our attention and attraction to the mental image we've created in our mind, attracting us to people, resources, and opportunities we need to achieve our goal.

Create a Frequency to Attract What You Want

There is a saying: what you focus on expands, good or bad. What do you want to focus on and what outcomes do you want in your life? Your thoughts create your outcomes. By believing this, you can take full responsibility for your life and all that happens in it. I'm no scientist by any stretch and there is a body of science I suggest you investigate to know more about this whole phenomenon of the power of thoughts and attraction frequency – and how, when these thoughts are attached to feelings, they create the outcome for whatever you are constantly thinking about. It compels my own thinking on this, for my life and for what I wish to share and demonstrate with others to be proactive with designing life for better, for creating a frequency from thoughts, to attract what you want, not what you don't want. This body of science includes psychology and neuroscience/quantum physics, and its major contributors such as Sigmund Freud, Neils Bohr and Albert Einstein and later contributors such as Ralph Waldo Emerson, Dr. John Hagelin, to name a few. In the professional working world, experts in their field such as Stephen Covey and Jack Canfield have been instrumental in demonstrating the profound benefits of this perspective for achieving progress and results.

The Frequency of Thoughts and Energy Vibrations

When you recall the great inventions of the world, they all started from thoughts. Consider Benjamin Franklin and his creative experiments to prove electricity and its uses or his invention of bifocals; to Thomas Edison and his creations of devices in fields such as electric power generation, motion pictures, and sound recording; to Alexander Graham Bell and his invention of the first practical telephone. Thoughts exist within every single human being; and every single human being is made up of energy. Thoughts, therefore, are measurable units of energy which are made up of biochemical electrical impulses that trigger physiological and emotional responses from your body in response to those impulses. Each time you think a thought, or a series of repetitive thoughts, you trigger your emotions and your response. The frequency of these thoughts to trigger the responsive action is charged by your feelings; and when thoughts and feelings are combined, your actions and frequency to produce an outcome will result. For instance, a client, Sally mentioned to me that, for years, while grateful, she has been bearing the guilt that her husband left his job to take care of their two toddlers so that she could focus on her career as an executive at a major investment firm. In these years of guilt, she rarely came home in time for dinner with her family, often missing even the bedtime tuck-ins. Through her personal transformation work with me, she realized that her focus had been on the guilt of her career advancement, which contradicted what she had really wanted which was balanced time for her family and her career. So what kept showing up was more of her not seeing her kids, more feelings of inadequacy as a loving parent, and more career advancement that brought about more work, more challenges, and time away from the home. Today, her focus is on reorganizing her work, eliminating unnecessary work, and replacing her negative feelings with positive feelings, engaging her team by delegating work that her team finds meaningful. The outcome within the year of her implementation is more balanced time with family, for self, better team engagement at work, and guilt-free to enjoy her moments of harmony and love.

To keep your energy vibrations in the same frequency, you have to manage your thoughts and emotions to align with what you want, not what you don't want. Take for instance a movie on Netflix you want to watch. Would you turn your television on and program it to ABC or a television network? No. You would program it to Netflix. Or, let's say you want to listen to an all-news station on the radio, but you tune your radio to a music station. Clearly, you won't get all the news you wanted. That's how it works: like attracting like, and cause and effect.

The Power of Creating Frequency to Attract What You Want

From my experience, I've discovered that being a deliberate thinker for what I want in my life (not what I don't want) helps to align me to the frequency of attracting what I want. From my view, to be a deliberate thinker, you engage in the conscious process of initiating an action to a focus on something you purposely think about, and then look for a solution to that specific matter or challenge. To be a deliberate thinker to achieve something you want, it requires repetitive thoughts which creates habits. Your emotional attraction to the thought is what creates the repetition of those thoughts in your mind which in turn forms a belief – which in turn, unleashes action.

There are three key and powerful universal laws for attracting what you want, within the context of setting the right frequency from your thoughts, feelings, and energy vibrations. They are: The Law of Cause and Effect, The Law of Least Effort, and The Law of Attraction. Simply put, the Law of Cause and Effect says that every action we take produces a force of energy that comes back to us with the same force. The Law of Least Effort says that all things natural (including human beings) naturally function with ease, harmony, and love; and when we harness the force of harmony and love, we create success and good for self and all, with little effort. Things like grass growing with ease, or taking a breath unconsciously are examples of this. The Law of Attraction (and as I've alluded to earlier) says that whatever you think about, talk about, and focus on, you will create more of in your life, especially those things you have intense feelings about.

So, when you're thinking and talking about how bad your situation is, you're going to create more bad situations in your life. We attract toward each other and things that are in the same frequency of our thoughts and feelings. Experts have proven that every thought we think, every feeling we feel, sends out a vibration that attracts the same thoughts and feelings. Quantum Physicist, Dr. John Hagelin, posits that the forcefield of a thought is the square of the number of people thinking that thought. This means that if two people were thinking the same repetitive thought, the power of the forcefield of that thought would be four; if four people were thinking the same thought, it would be sixteen. So, if more people were aligned with the same repetitive thought, think about what could be realized for engagement with achieving results. Imagine what you could do with this theory for you and for those you lead.

When you think about the framing needed for leaders to solve problems (and its many inherent dilemmas, systems/framework, your own inner make-up), you can understand why your mindset is such a critical foundation for what outcomes show up in your life and how you will approach succeeding in anything you put your mind to. When you think about how you will turn things around for your tired, near-disengaged team members so that aligned results can be achieved for targets you're on the hook for, think about how it starts with you and your clarity of focus. Think about how your "problem" is really a part of your gap from current state to future state – the gap that needs your priority focus; the gap that includes your mindset and influences your experience in the workplace, in relationships, in your personal life. Think about your gap as an opportunity for realizing great potential.

French psychotherapist Emile Coue introduced auto-suggestion into his practice to teach his clients how to heal themselves. He posited that repetition of positive thinking contributes significantly to self-healing. His mantra was, "every day, and in every way, I am becoming better and better."

I introduce this concept with clients by illustrating that thinking in a certain way (cause) influences actions (effect), which in turn produces the outcome. What they discover are new ways of thinking from realizing language they use that don't serve their right focus, statements such as, "I've never been good with presenting to a large group," or "I can't do that, X will never allow it," or "I should be…" or "What you teach will never work for me or my team…our industry doesn't work that way," or "I'm so overwhelmed, this is the last thing I need on my plate." With statements like this, you give yourself more of what you just said, not the solution. Reframing statements like these to attract what you do want is a fundamental step to getting into the right mindset so that you have specific clarity of your current state, your desired end state, and the gap where you can work on your solution path. When you have this picture in mind, you can get going effectively with your solution path because you've just brought your end goal into your present way of thinking.

Think of your mindset as an "activater" for achieving your success (what I cover with my clients). Think of you – a great leader – who lives, embodies and demonstrates the value of:

- Awareness from a growth and creative mindset
- Clarity of and commitment to purpose and vision
- Taking time to tidy up your thoughts and emotions to maximize energy
- Influencing your outcomes through response-ability
- Vibrating the values that guide you to what you want through and through
- Action from accountability and the right goals
- Talk the talk, walk the walk – being the person that supports what you say
- Empowering self, enabling others toward their self-empowerment
- Relationships that matter and attract success

Chapter 5:

ACTIONS THAT MAKE SUCCESS STICK

"It had long since come to my attention that people of accomplishment rarely sat back and let things happen to them. They went out and happened to things."
– Leonardo de Vinci

R ewards that come from success are through the right actions taken. The right actions that stick to success are those actions that reveal themselves through your deliberate thinking of and committed efforts to achieving your vision, your goal, your purpose. We may know this, but it's surprising how many people get stuck in thoughts and activities that don't really stick to success. Knowledge is all good for the information you need to know for whatever it is you want to attend to. But for knowledge to manifest into the success you want to achieve, you must feel the love, joy, and connection for the results you want to achieve, and from these, take action. It's taking action that activates the physical realization of whatever you've learned from informational sources and from your own clarity of your goal/ objective, to realize success.

From personal experience, I find many often do things (take action), grasping to a routine that doesn't enable a conscious calibration or recalibration of the decision or motive behind the action. Or, we may think we're not achieving anything, yet we are, but it's the same stuff we don't want in our life. So how do we get ourselves to take the right action so that it sticks to what we do want in our life, to achieve success? The answer is this: condition your consciousness to deliberately create positive thoughts that will make you act forward, not act by default to "same old same", or to the belief you can control the past. The past is done, and when you act from thinking you can control the past, it gets you results that don't serve your end goal. Select those thoughts that open your mind to possibilities that connect you to your heart in the context of gratitude, joy, and love. When you strengthen your consciousness in this way, you re-program your subconscious mind – the part of your brain that shapes your thoughts into beliefs. Beliefs are what influence your behaviour, which translate to actions.

Why Are Beliefs Important to Action?

Beliefs are important because they are what create our behaviour, and behaviour is important because it's what triggers the actions we take. To make actions stick to success, beliefs must align with what you set out to accomplish. Think about it, every action you take (including the display of your emotions, rational or irrational) have come from the beliefs you have, whether you know it consciously or not. For example, you brush your teeth, because you were told by your dentist that brushing is good for your teeth and your health and you believe it. You may test it, and not brush your teeth, and when you get that cavity and/or gum malaise, you then accept what your dentist says, and you're back to regularly brushing your teeth.

From what I've learned through neuroscience and psychology studies and from personal experience, a belief is formed by a repetitive thought that your conscious part of your mind has accepted to be true, and this thought gets stored in the subconscious part of your mind. Basically, when your mind feels a thought is acceptable to store for future reference, that same thought repeats itself and enters your subconscious as a belief. This belief is applied for intellectual purposes as well as for action purposes. For instance, if you hold the belief that it's bad luck when a black cat crosses your path, then your intellect (knowledge) says "It's bad luck when a black cat crosses your path." That same belief is applied for action purposes when you purposefully avoid any black cat on the street, because you hold that belief.

Beliefs also involve emotion, which motivates you to act. So, in this black-cat belief example, you were motivated to avoid all black cats on the street because of your feeling that bad luck will come your way. This brings me to another point about certain beliefs, the kind that make us superstitious. Superstitions as I know them to be are as real as one creates them to be. Some say that superstition is designated to those beliefs that result from ignorance and fear of the unknown. An example of a personal superstition that comes to mind for me is my favourite hoody which I believe gives me good luck. I aced an important telephone interview with a prospective client while wearing it. And just recently while wearing it, I wrote and sent in my application to write this book with a book agent, and bam…! Regardless of what anyone says, if the belief makes you feel good and do good (remember, mind-heart connection), I say believe away. My point is this, if your belief motivates you enough to evoke inspiration for you to move and act with mind-heart connection and it serves you and others from your best self, that's a belief in action you'll want to pay attention to having more of. Now, if you need more incentive to be excited by this as a possibility for you, here's another fascinating revelation I found through the neuroscience research available about neuroplasticity (Google it and read up for yourself): our brain is not a static organ and is malleable. What does this mean? It means that our brain has the ability to reorganize itself physically and functionally, regardless of our age and due to the environment in which we live, the thoughts we think, our behaviour, and our management of emotions. Guess who unleashes that ability for our brain – each of us! You can actually re-wire your brain's capability so that the thoughts you think, the beliefs you acquire from your thoughts, the resulting behaviours you formed from thoughts, the consequential emotions you attach to your beliefs and behaviour, and the actions you take as a result of all this, can change and align with what you set out to achieve for yourself. All this happens because you will it, by deliberate, conscious choice. I feel it important at this stage to share with you a side-note: this re-wiring business takes time and some processing effort (yes, actions), unique to each individual; and for some, deeper, more expert-level support (such as a psychotherapist) may be required. Why? Because if you've never re-wired your thinking, consciously, before, there's likely work to be done around discovering past influences on your current brain's thoughts, beliefs, and associated emotions that may surprise you. This, in turn, could also bring up a high emotional charge for you that requires attention and processing. In addition, old habits will need to be replaced by new ones that support the re-wiring, which means you will need to take the time to take new actions, practice them, until they become a habit. This side-note is not intended to scare you. It is to make you aware that achieving greatness takes time and effort. In fact, when you tap into the great limitless potential to self-heal and to achieve meaningful success from within, you will quickly experience the progressive forward movement of your personal success transformation which acts as a solid base for all other successes you want to achieve. Think about this as you shape your personal strategy for taking action, and for engaging your team in a lasting way.

Taking action is an act of faith of what you believe – it is a demonstrated statement that you believe that something is going to happen. Knowing what actions stick to success are critical to ensuring you reach your goals.

Actions That Come from Inspiration

While there are obvious actions that need to be taken such as acquiring the educational credentials for a technical capability (what business-speak calls the "hard skills" such as job/field of expertise – a doctor, for instance, requiring a medical degree and an area of specialization learning credentials to specialize), there are also actions that come from inspiration and from the heart that are critical for success.

When you have the inspiration to do something, act on it to shift your life to opportunities that may not have appeared, had you not acted on your inspiration. That happened to a client of mine. Susan had this inspiring idea she shared with me, that she had put some thought to but didn't get around to taking action. She explained that a year later, a colleague of hers ran with the same inspiring idea and is now generating the revenue Susan had dreamed of having. Have you ever had an idea that you hadn't acted on and then you find someone else had the same idea, took action on it, and successfully changed their life?

Here are seven actions that I suggest to my clients to schedule in their day for shifting and reinforcing beliefs that make actions into habits that stick to success:

Morning gratitude / meditation (five minutes dedication, or sprinkle this into your morning activity, e.g., when brushing your teeth, walking your dog, making breakfast, etc.) – identify what you are grateful for, from the moment you wake up, mentally (or verbally) call out what you appreciate that you are noticing around you as you are doing your regular morning routine.

Settling in time at the office (usually half- to one hour before your first meeting) – no interactions, just review your day's schedule, grab that hot or cold beverage, and set your mindset with positive affirmations for the kind of day you will want to have:

Lunch break – commit to this! Start with a half-hour of dedicated time to have a meal, savour it, and nourish your body with nutrients it needs:

Afternoon break time – take a minimum of 15 minutes for break time from work activity. Reboot your mind by doing something that takes your mind away from your work activity (e.g., leave your desk and chat with a colleague over a cup of tea/coffee; close your eyes at your desk and call out what you're grateful for in your life, meditate)

Personal Relationships time – make room after work, at dinner and bed time routine/tuck in for those with children. Engage in something that takes your mind away from work and deadlines (e.g., conversation with your spouse and/or kids about their day; call a friend)

Throughout the day – ensure five actions are taken by day's end that serve personal purpose goals (e.g, self-care, practice of new learned habit, gratitude, journal thoughts of joy, list negative feelings you will process to release in a healthy way and what you will replace it with, actions toward any of your stated goals)

Before you go to bed – take a minimum of 10 minutes for gratitude and mindset clearing/heart-mind intention for the next day. In this, I suggest time to reflect on the day and what you are grateful for the past (grateful for the good and bad that happened – if bad, reframe to what was grateful about it), present moment gratitude (what they are feeling at this very moment and how they feel in mind, body, heart, to be grateful for – here I recommend being grateful for an 'as-if-in-the-future' scenario to reinforce their intention for next day and for their future vision goals and intentions)

Actions That Attract and Serve Purpose and Goals

In today's world of abundance and opportunity, it's amazing that almost everything we have ever wanted to do or have, has already been done or had by someone else. As Jack Canfield says, "Success leaves clues". Whether it's writing a best-selling book, losing weight, running a marathon, improving relationships, becoming financially independent, getting a dream job, starting a movement, or leading a successful business – there is someone out there who has already done it and has left clues for us, available in person, on the internet, online courses, through books and manuals, seminars, and coaching. Take the action of leveraging these clues and don't think your show-stopping obstacle is because you must start from scratch all on your own. Go see that person who's been there and done it, go on the internet, take that course/seminar, buy that book or manual, sign up for coaching with that person. Gain the knowledge you need from them. And then apply your learnings, practice them, shift current thoughts and behaviours to align with them, and take the actions you need toward the success you want.

Actions are activities that accomplish an objective. If the objective is not clear, the actions taken are merely distractions that either need to be eliminated, addressed, or adjusted, starting with the action of clarifying the real objective. Alice, a client of mine, learned this. She stated that a goal/objective was to renew her business brand so that she could improve her revenue and needed help with this. She had been impressed with my business mission statement and thought to meet with me for some advice. I welcomed a meeting, which turned out to be an "aha" moment for her. The branding topic took all of 15 minutes of our time together while the rest of the hour was spent helping her through some difficult emotions for her that came up. Alice had spent three years in her business where she would, at times during each year, peak to achieving sales she was pleased with, and then for the majority of the year, she would find herself with little energy and motivation to consistently generate sales for meaningful revenue goals, let alone interact with people that could help her achieve more sales. As a result, she was living from the profits gained until she was in a scrambling position to generate more sales. She had initially rationalized this to a lack of branding for business, to target high-paying clients. Through our discussion, she realized her pattern of how her handling of her business and life was incongruent to the goal she stated she wanted to achieve. We explored her feelings through this pattern, and she explained that since her divorce a few years prior, she had been feeling as though she could do nothing right in her life. She had family members constantly telling her to "get a real job", giving her advice that was only adding to her self-doubt and low self-esteem. By the end of that initial session, she realized that before she could take consistent actions for her goal of increased sales, the brand strategy she needed to work on was the source of her brand: her Self. Within a year of working with her through this, Alice took right actions from clear objectives and is now setting in motion her business goals, while continuing her personal goals for mindset wellness, in support of taking right actions in her life.

Solutions-Oriented Actions

When you stick to thinking that there's a problem needing to be solved, that's what you get: more problems to solve. The word "problem" just gets into the skin of my heart and mind-space that life is about problems that just have to be solved. Yuck! How is that exciting? In this heart and mind-space connection, I've tended to find myself frozen and giving up or postponing action. I react and what I find is that I create more of what I don't want showing up in my life. I see this happening for others too. It's kind of like you knowing you have house chores, like that cabinet drawer that just won't close because you've jammed every little trinket in it. And then, you need something you can't find so you look in that drawer rummaging through it with no luck of finding what you're looking for. So you close it right back to the extent it will allow you, only now, you realize you just found another problem you have to deal with, getting that darn drawer cleaned out. And maybe that's all it takes to set your day in motion, to believing it's going to be a bad day, one problem after another.

For many faced with problems, it's easy to retreat and not face them. But what if you find yourself closer to achieving what it is you want, if you take action to resolve those problems? What if those problems are success clues in a gap that, when tended to, actually gives you possibilities for catapulting you to your breakthrough goals? Perhaps the only thing stopping you from taking action towards achieving results you want is because of your perspective and not knowing what to consider and what actions to take. Here is another thing, though. Sometimes, it's just about taking action, seizing the momentum of deliberately doing something for the sake of results you want. That clean drawer may not be enough to inspire you to clean it up; but the end result (when you're clear on what that is, such as being able to find things), is all it takes for you to take action.

Some years ago, my life partner at the time, Geoff, an ex-Airborne veteran, was into skydiving as a hobby of his that he'd wanted me to be a part of. It was costing us a wad of money and with him having left the military on my request (yes, I was madly in love, but I was not military-wife material) and just starting a new boring job, I knew we couldn't sustain the sport long-term. But Geoff needed a sport he could enjoy, and I wanted to be part of something with him. After a few sky-dives under my belt, and as super-exciting as it was, I realized skydiving wasn't something I could see myself doing long-term, and since it was also a costly sport even for just one of us to maintain, I looked into other thrill sports that were less expensive and interesting enough for both of us. Rock climbing became the option. The only problem was that I wasn't sure I had the physical aptitude for it. Yes, all doubts and fears rushed in. When I researched more, I got more intrigued about the idea of rock climbing and how it could be something both of us could enjoy while meeting our balanced thrill-seeking needs.

After our indoor climb training for about a year, we loved it so much we decided to take our newfound love outdoors. My favourite type of climbing was top-roping (a form of climbing where the rope is already threaded through an anchor at the top of the route, and a person belays from the ground to control the rope while you're climbing the route). For years, we'd set off for our expeditions in the summer sea-sons to hit every corner of Ontario's trails leading to cliffs and escarp-ments. The preparation included making sure we had our tent gear, food and water supplies, climbing gear, warm clothing, scheduled time off from work, and lots and lots of stamina and courage. Making a list and gathering for what we needed materially was simple enough; this whole thing about a fearless gut (as Geoff would often remind me) that required having the mental stamina and calm nerves for this adventure. I wasn't sure I had it in me. Every climb trip that involved a riskier type of climbing – called traditional-style climbing (or "trad" climbing) required me to 'psyche' myself that I could do it. In trad climbing, climbers would place their climbing tools into the climb route to protect against falls and remove them when a climbing pitch was complete.

With the indoor training I knew what it took to be safe, but my gut was still not fearless (it was more like a gelatin with annoying butterflies flitting about in there). My frame of mind had to be spot on before every trip so I tapped into my regimen of Tai Chi and meditation. This helped significantly with calming my fears, anxiety, and with mind-body flow. Each climbing feat had its variables for safety, thrill, and high nerves, which finished off by a heart-stopping rappel down the limestone, lichen covered escarpment that we just scaled and conquered. My highest trad-climb and rappel was 350 feet, Mazinaw cliff, at Bon Echo in southeast Ontario, which took us an average of seven hours to climb.

When I look back at this, the challenge was making sure our will, focus, and capability to climb and rappel were all in check. I set a goal to join my partner on a sport and chunked my action steps down to what I could handle each step of the way, until I reached my goal. Were there times that I thought I'd poop my pants in midst of climbing a steep cliff? You bet. I learned so much physically, mentally, and emotionally. What sticks out is that heart and mind had everything to do with determining if I was going to plough through the action steps to my goal – climb with my husband, and make sure I wasn't a "wuss" in the process. What I got out of it, I will never forget, and I can apply what I've learned in all areas of my life.

If you want something, don't think about your situation as a problem, think about it as a challenge that has opportunity for a solution – be solution-oriented. You want to feel and see in your heart-and-mind's eye just how great it would be to breaking-through that challenge. In this way, your heart and mind are connected, and your body follows to action steps that are right for you. These action steps will also stretch you to rise to your occasion, for meaningful results – for success. Everything you think about creates your reality. So why not focus on what thoughts it will take to create the reality you want.

Ever since Rhonda Byrne's *The Secret* came out (book and movie), I've been so fascinated by the concept of the law of attraction and how it relates to achieving success. This book led me to other like-minds like Wallace Wattles and his book collection The Complete Wallace D. Wattles 9 Books: A Timeless Wisdom Collection Book that helped me to personalize the law of attraction. Can I just say, for me, the law of attraction is bang on?! I came across more other like-minds who have brilliantly captivated me with delicious concepts and principles I use in my own life and in my approach to helping others. One such like-minded soul who expanded my understanding of natural and universal laws was Deepak Chopra. In his book, The Seven Spiritual Laws of Success, he posits that there are seven natural and universal laws that ignite the "spirit" to achieve success: the law of pure potentiality, the law of giving, the law of cause and effect, the law of least effort, the law of intention and desire, the law of detachment, and the law of purpose in life. The principles of these laws have been woven into my personal and professional approach to authentic success both personally and professionally.

The heart (spirit) of success is truly personal, and the way to reaching that success (authentic to you) is through your thoughts and feelings, your mind and heart, connected and aligned. When you can tap into that spirit you become a deliberate thinker and you'll open possess the power to create whatever it is you want, not just what you don't want.

Actions for Forward Momentum – Big and Small

To engage others, you must yourself be engaged. You must feel it, act it, live it, and model it from the inside-out. Coming from a Human Resources background partnering with various businesses (both in for-profit and not-for-profit sectors) I've collaborated on many strategies (development, implementation, and support for both leader and non-management staff) for what it takes to make a business successful through its people. I've always been a firm believer that one of the simplest and most important secrets to success in any discipline is right action, right away. I've noticed that success often starts when we make ourselves open to opportunities in the context of love and are willing to do what it takes to act on that success.

Through my certification in training the Success Principles™ by Jack Canfield, I guide my clients on key success habits, one which demonstrates that when we lean into taking action aligned with our purpose even in the absence of a full plan, it's a leap of faith which leads to the next actions needed toward reaching the goal we've set.

In the absence of a plan, there are levels of engagement that are as simple as just seizing what we intuitively consider as doing the right things. A long, detailed plan is not needed – just taking action for forward motion can make a difference. Leadership is essentially about prompt, responsible, and committed decision-making that creates and inspires consistent action producing the inspired results that permeates to others. This, in turn, creates consistent action. There isn't much procrastinating or over-thinking things. Research shows that a habit of successful people is simply trying different approaches until they find one that works for them. As Woody Allen was once noted to have said, "80% of success is showing up." Some people often look at successful people and wonder how and why they became so successful. It's because they simply chose to take action, to seize their moments for great possibilities, and just take action. There wasn't any distracting chit-chat, no wishful thinking without follow-through, no overthinking, no over-planning or control. More often than not, they just took a step, right into action.

Actions towards a goal: Try this today or tomorrow, and see how it works for you:

Choose something within what you believe is in your reach and take action immediately. If you feel you can't choose something, think again until you come up with something you feel is within your reach.

Catch yourself when you get triggered to negative feelings of fear or wishful thinking without follow through action – and try again, choose something to reach and take action.

Don't fuss, worry, and spiral into defeat (big or small) if your idea isn't 100% perfect. A little advice here, it will never be perfect, and you'll have the chance to refine more accurately as you go, anyway.

Don't forget to be open to different outcomes and to relax and enjoy the productivity of just doing something for the sake of productivity, whatever that healthily means to you.

Choose, choose all the time, and learn from your choices, even if you don't get the result you want, you can learn from your experience.

One of the biggest actions to take that's often not leveraged is to ask (to understand, clarify, to get support, to improve from feedback and new information).

Be specifically grateful, every chance you get in your day. Be grateful for the past, the present, and the hopeful promising future. Describe what it is you're grateful for, in detail. This will create the mental image you need to shift your mindset to positive thinking and visualization of positive possibilities.

Love, love, love, every moment of your day. This can only bring more love and joy to receive and give, which opens your mind and heart for limitless positive possibilities.

I'm a thousand percent certain that by taking action and doing something now, no matter how small, you will feel positive, enthused, and energized. Try it.

Seven Leadership Skills that Increase Engagement

With 25 years of workplace experience and learnings, I've learned that there are at least five essential skills at the personal dimension level that leaders must have, and take action to demonstrate, if they're going to succeed in increasing engagement. They are:

Building Trust

Trust is an essential ingredient for increasing engagement. The first thing leaders need to know about building trust is that it doesn't happen just because you think you are trustworthy. People do not know how trustworthy you are until you demonstrate it through trust building behaviours and the most important of these behaviours is to trust others. This requires a basic belief in people, a belief that people are essentially trustworthy. After all, if your employees are not trustworthy, why did you hire them and why are they still there?

Mentoring

The relationship between the employee and their immediate manager is a critical factor for how engaged the employee will be. We have to get away from the idea that managers cannot mentor the people who report to them. The Gallup research is very clear on this point. Employees need feedback, they need to know how to discover their part in navigating through challenges at work and creating and being part of solutions (not just identify problems). They need to know how they are performing regularly, not just once a year at review time, and not just about bottom-line business results. They need to learn and know about what affects their motivation to perform effectively. They need to be able to discuss their needs for growth and development, and their challenges with a manager who cares empathically about them. A manager who cares about their employees are effective leaders that know how to give and receive authentic feedback and to coach and counsel employees in a way that increases engagement and commitment – because they know what it feels like to be engaged and committed, from the inside-out. A manager who can mentor, is a manager who shows leadership, because they also do their inner work.

Meaningful Involvement

Whether employees feel like an insider or an outsider (sense of belonging or non-belonging with the organization) also impacts their level of engagement. Effective leaders know that everyone on their team has strengths the team needs, and they know how to get the best out of each person. They understand that people with different personal values can work together effectively when they commit to the same values about trustworthiness and standards of work performance.

Alignment and Clear Accountability and Latitude to Make Decisions

Engaged employees feel aligned with their organization's purpose, values and vision. Their work is meaningful to them because their leader helps them see the connection between what they do and the success of the organization. The effective leader also understands that gaining their team's commitment to the organization's values increases the team's performance standards as well as their engagement.

Individual and Team Development (Personal and Professional)

Effective leaders understand the potential for significant increases in performance through high performing teams. They make sure that all team members understand the strengths and passions they and other team members bring to the team and work at developing a process that leverages from these strengths. The leader's focus is on developing the leadership potential of each team member and ultimately implementing a shared leadership approach to continuously improving performance that is owned by the team. To add to this, including a more wholistic approach by incorporating personal transformation, you can make a true difference and sustain high engagement while maximizing a healthy self-sufficiency with higher emotional intelligence and resilience for handling inevitable challenges.

All these skills are needed to fully engage employees. Engagement will be diminished if any of them are missing. The challenge in developing these skills is that they are dependent on each other. That is, you must build trust before you can be effective at mentoring and you will need your mentoring skills to be effective at inclusion and alignment. You won't have much success at getting your team aligned unless they feel connected to themselves and to the organization.

The reality is that these skills don't come naturally to many managers and leaders, and yet they can be learned. Extensive research by Daniel Goleman, author of Primal Leadership and expert in emotional intelligence, has established that they cannot be learned during a single training event. Developing these skills will, for many managers require the unlearning of old habits – often habits formed over a lifetime – and the learning of new habits. It takes time, personal reinforcement, practice, and a serious commitment from both the organization and the manager involved.

With all the evidence we now have about the significant increases in organizational performance as employee engagement increases, can anyone afford not to make the effort?

Making Right Decisions and Choices

Connect your decisions with your heart – your heart is where your intentions live. When your mind is connected with your heart, the right thoughts will come out and the power of those thoughts will keep you to your intention. The power of your thoughts is strong and produces outcomes. It's your thoughts which determine if the outcome is good or bad. Choose positive thoughts that are in keeping with your intention. Your positive thoughts will also attract like-mind-hearted people. Here's something interesting, Dr. John Hagelin (physicist) posits that the power of a forcefield of a thought is the square root of the number of people thinking the same thought. Think about it, people come together in their churches because of their beliefs – repetitive thoughts that hold their faith. Imagine in your organization, you have thoughts that attract one team member. That's two of you now with the same thoughts. Now imagine four of you. That's 16 with the same thoughts. Now imagine 10 of you. That's 100 of you with the same thoughts. You need to engage through your thoughts – a powerful tool to action out!

So, you want to put more time into leadership-related activities – things like coaching, mentoring, and developing your team, listening, inspiring, and establishing a strategic vision. It starts with whether you can practice this for your own self-development from the inside-out.

The Value of Meaningful Goals-Setting and Planning

Once there is clarity of purpose, vision, and needs and desires are identified, it's important to translate them into goals and objectives that are SMART (specific, meaningful, achievable, results-focused, and time-bound); otherwise, what we want to achieve stays as an idea or dream and will not be realized until we release it into action. Experts on the science of personal success, neuroscience (particularly in the study of neuroplasticity) confirm that the brain is a goal-seeking organ. Whatever goal we set and lay out, our brain supports to set in motion for us to achieve. Setting goals and objectives is a powerful process for thinking about your ideal future state and what action needs to be considered for achieving that future state. The process of setting goals and objectives will help you to choose where you want to go, motivate you because you have set the intention to achieve them, guide you on what actions it takes to get there, and will hold you and your team accountable for achieving what you say you want.

Another important thing about goals is that they have to be compelling enough for you that you will want to commit to achieving them.

Setting breakthrough goals – those goals that are beyond your comfort zone such as "BHAG" (big, hairy, audacious goals) is one powerful way that catapults you into action, because these goals compel you to rise above what you are today. When I work with my clients, I draw from my certified teachings of Canfield's Success Principles, and guide them through this concept by having them establish seven breakthrough goals, one for each of the seven key aspects in life that many of us aspire successes in:

- Financial – e.g. income, profit, cashflow, net worth, investments, debt reduction
- Business/Career – e.g. dream job, entrepreneur ventures
- Relationships – e.g. family, friends, romantic, colleagues
- Body/Health/Fitness – e.g. body weight, body image, nutrition/diet, exercise
- Recreation/Leisure/Fun Time – e.g. recreational activities, travel, vacation, hobbies, sports
- Personal – e.g. possessions, purchases, education, spiritual growth, personal development, experiences
- Contribution/Legacy – e.g. philanthropy, legacy, volunteer service, community
- For each of these aspects, my clients work through identifying:
- Vision (clearly stated)
- Goals and objectives (how much and by when) for the vision
- Affirmation statements that reinforce the achievement of goals and vision with positive feelings (e.g. "I'm so happy and grateful that I now have…"), and
- Stated next steps of actions to take – for each vision

By taking consistent action on a daily basis, with clarity of purpose, and in the context of love and joy, you will see that over time your efforts will accumulate into greater results. Whether it's with personal growth, professional growth…small, significant changes and shifts in aligning your mindset to serving your purpose and goals through right actions, which lead to amazing results that permeate from within you to your life environments and to a connection with others that makes a true difference.

Chapter 6:

COMMITMENT WITH ACCOUNTABILITY

"There is a difference between interest and commitment.
When you're interested in doing something, you do it only when
it's convenient. When you're committed to something,
you accept no excuses, only results."
– Ken Blanchard, *The One Minute Manager*

A Matter of Integrity: Hold True to Your Intentions and Agreements

When we believe in something enough to go beyond the challenges and obstacles we face, we are demonstrating commitment with accountability, and this is important for acting with integrity, for demonstrating your integrity. Case in point, writing this book in flow. I hadn't realized that I'd be going through writer's block when it was the last thing I needed at the time: Two hours before I was to get ready for a four-hour training and coaching session with a client. This would put me behind and I desperately wanted a good early night's rest. I'd composed myself and managed to get it together by remembering my intentions and goals to keep to my agreements, so I put aside my writing, prepared for my client, and after the mutually meaningful session, I resumed writing, and joyfully, at that. Though an exhausting day and having to pull an all-nighter, I felt proudly accomplished for staying committed with finishing my writing goal milestone and meeting my client's needs. I accepted that sometimes, that's just what it takes, with no regrets and much to gain.

It's a simple enough concept that when you are committed to what you set out to achieve, you will do what it takes to achieve the outcome. Yet, it's surprising how many of us wake up each day kicking and screaming with ourselves over whether or not to keep our commitments, stick to our disciplines, or carry out our action plans. Whether your goal is a personal or professional one (or both), 100% commitment, no excuses, is what it takes to achieve it. In the personal experience I shared earlier about keeping my commitments to my written book and to my client during my writer's block fiasco, we were working on her goal to how to stop feeling guilty all the time, and one of the pieces of wisdom I drew from was Byron Katie's concept of "doing the work." It's basically taking a belief that's making us unhappy, examining it to see how true the belief is, qualifying it, and seeing if there's another way of thinking about it. My client looked at me, and her immediate response (shoulders drooped, big sigh) was, "I get what you're saying, but that sounds like a lot of work, and I'm already feeling overwhelmed from the thought of it." It was only our third coaching session together. I suggested she trust her true purpose and accept where she was at as a natural part of the process. I also reminded her that, if you love your purpose, you'll commit to the work and may even surprise yourself with finding more to love through the work. It then got me to thinking of some of my other clients who were farther along in their process with this concept of "doing the work." They were demonstrating having done the work, feeling engaged and continuing to do the work: eating healthy, finding balance in their use of time, quality relationships, living active lifestyles. They invested time to be flexible and to work on mindset, balance, and inner work so that they could unleash their positive habits and therefore reaping one successful result after another. These people released the thinking and behaving that did not serve their wellbeing. They were continuing to see how thinking and behaving from a place of centredness, clarity of purpose, and focus, have brought them success in achieving what they set out to achieve. They did and are doing the work required through 100% commitment, knowing full well it takes work and dedication, but just as equally reaping the benefits of feeling the liberation from it – the liberation of more time to be with those they love, more time for self-care, working smarter, being more present to enjoy and love life, rather than living a life bound by senseless to-do lists, an overbooked calendar, an overloaded headspace of negative self-talk or whatever fills it that's causing self-sabotage. Doing the work from the inside out and staying committed to it is like all goals you want to achieve because you're in love with that vision of reaching them. It brings you more energy, creativity, and freedom to think, behave and act from a place of peace, centeredness, purpose, and love. There is a freedom from knowing oneself, and from that knowledge creating and realizing a profound sense that anything is achievable if you set your mind to it from this place of self-knowing.

When we keep our commitments, we then hold on to our integrity and we do what we say we are going to do. The value we place on that commitment has no conditions except that the commitment is kept. The measure of that value is what makes it different from what Ken Blanchard refers to as "interest." With interest, there is an exception, an out-clause we convince ourselves is valid – typically in the form of an excuse to get out of keeping the commitment. With commitment, there are no exceptions, no excuses, no convenience. You do what it takes because you love the vision of reaching that goal. How many times do we find ourselves breaking a commitment we've made? Ask yourself if you've done this and you'll probably come up with your reasons that validated yourself permission to break them. A quick sure-fire tip to keep your commitments is to make only those commitments you're sure you can and really want to keep. After all, a commitment means you are dedicated to holding to what you say will do, without exception, because it matters that much to you.

Time Management to Commitment Management

As I mentioned earlier, an organization's time is ongoing, and in reality, you can never change the fact that you only have X amount of time in a work day, and you have priorities outside that of the organization. So, really, it's not about managing time. It's about you are managing, what you put into that time. Choosing the right commitments is a first step to what you put into your time. Second step is to prioritize what you put into your time, based on what Stephen Covey refers to as those "big rocks." – scheduling those important priorities that our roles play in our life that matter – time spent on key relationships and responsibilities, important projects, critical meetings. I would also suggest time spent on you (your mindset, emotional and physical wellness).

Commitment Prioritization

What do you prioritize as your leadership commitments? An engagement zapper is prioritizing those things that satisfy only one part of your life. You immerse yourself, by choice, to the life environments you choose to participate in, where you lovingly and joyfully express your passion, purpose, and talents. Each environment (business, personal, and home) progresses with you in it. Each has a whole system/framework to be carried out with principles, disciplines, and processes, and you have aspirations/desires within each. When you have a solid clear purpose of knowing yourself in these systems, you're in a position to be able to know what to prioritize based on the value of your interests and commitments you set to them. But you won't know this if you don't know your true authentic self and what you value – do the inner work and you'll be crystal clear.

Know Your Commitments and Stick to Them

When you're clear on your goal purpose (rooted from self-knowing and true purpose – that inner work), it's also important to learn to say no, as guided by your priorities you're committed to. Stop tending to stuff that doesn't serve your commitment or purpose.

Sometimes you won't be sure if you should tend to something as a priority. When it's not clear, gauge how you feel about it. If, for some reason, you feel compelled to do that something, it could be an inspired action that could lead you to unfolding a possibility that serves what you've set out. You must be open to this, but not to the point that you're back to that old habit of taking on everything that comes your way and wondering where the time went, causing you emotions and negative feelings that get the better of you. Check in with your motives for taking that something on.

Protect Your Personal Time and Try These Tips:

Set Boundaries for Your Day

It's easy to get sucked into being busy doing nothing, whether we know it or not at the time. Sometimes we just find ourselves checking the easy items off of our "to-do" list, and then we find ourselves checking the internet for research-turned-into-surfing the net for the latest update on international news or a vacation hot-spot; and there are times we have people pulling us in different directions. Either way, determining your most important activities and prioritizing them over those easy check off tasks will change your quality output and sense of balance in work and life for the better. Drawing from Stephen Covey's analogy of small "Big Rocks" in his Habit 3: Put First Things First® before anything else. Setting your boundaries requires demonstrating them, and being honest with others about your commitment to them.

Know What Is Really Important and Commit

Identifying your big rocks are easier said than done. For leaders, it can often feel that everything is a big rock. But you'll be surprised to know, it's really not. Utilize the 80/20 rule to help identify your big rocks. The 80/20 rule says that 80 percent of what you can impact will be from 20 percent of your actions, if they are the right ones. Therefore, identify those actions that lead to the greatest impact and put your focus there. Committing, by the way, simplifies your life because when you commit, there are no exceptions, no excuses. You just get it done.

Kill Perfectionism Before It Kills You

There is a saying that perfection is the enemy of done. It's also a killer to health, no lie. Recent studies in psychology have linked emotional-based mental health and physiological illnesses to perfectionism. Seriously, kill perfectionism.

Be Solutions-Oriented and Encourage This

Rather than finding problems in things, be solutions oriented. This keeps you committed to taking full responsibility for creating your outcomes by deliberate thinking when you run across challenges. Don't default to making excuses. An example of an excuse that creates more challenges is when we blame or complain about someone or something for why a problematic situation occurred. Blaming and complaining are not the same as identifying what has to be resolved – they are about making excuses that delay resolution, and create more to resolve. Ask yourself how often you find yourself creating your own obstacles in front of you. You can always find reasons not to do something. Maybe it keeps you comfy like a warm, safe blanket. By staying comfortable all the time, all you get are the same results. Maybe there's fear of something – a bruised ego, being exposed as incompetent, or self-doubt in your own abilities. You must realize that the knowledge you have today that got you to where you are at this moment, isn't likely going to get you to where you want to get to – or else you'd already be there. Also, to achieve what you have not yet achieved, you have to do something you've not done before and commit to it if you want to change your current reality.

One key to being solutions-oriented is to be flexible. Not everything goes as planned. You have to understand and be good enough at leadership to teach it to your employees, both by example and by coaching. The more leaders you can develop, the stronger the business will be, and the less you will have to worry about how the business is operating.

Another key is to embrace boundaries. Think about where you want to be one year from today. Be selective (if possible) with tasks and say "yes" to tasks that will help you align with where you want to be in the future. Say no to the things that will not support your growth or purpose, especially if you already have a lot on your plate, or carefully look at what's on your plate.

Another key is to trust. Trust your moments, the process you're going through, yourself, those around you, and that the world is not out to get you but to serve you through love. When you trust, you're able to find and leverage all that's great in the resources you have and need to resolve challenges that come your way. Trusting also helps you to leverage your core genius (skills and strengths) as well as others' – and from that, not only establish a trusting relationship but also increase engagement, productivity, morale, creativity for ideas and innovative thinking, and results.

Build the Right Supports for Success

Building the right support network for achieving success in anything is critical. For instance, to achieve maximum results, it's important to be constantly growing and learning with new ways of thinking, being, and doing. Asking for and using feedback from the right credible sources demonstrates your commitment to continuous improvements and to achieving our goals which move you further and faster toward achieving your goals.

Once you're clear on what it is you want, and you have a vision and goals to support, you can identify the core things you need to tend to, and it usually requires support from others. Remember that "success leaves clues". Without outside support, we tend to get stuck in doing things the same way we've always done them, or the same way everyone else in your circle or organization or field of expertise does. I've learned that by networking with people from different specialties, industries and/or professions, you can gain different perspectives and new ideas that you may not have thought of before. I've found that the concept of Mastermind Groups is one effective way you can help continue to think "outside the box," and maximize the generation of creative ideas and solutions that you may not necessarily have considered. Napoleon Hill discussed mastermind groups in his awesome book Think and Grow Rich, and from what I've learned it's a practice growing in popularity where people are crediting this type of group forum as having helped them significantly to be successful. Built on the foundation of trust, confidentiality, and focus, mastermind groups share the philosophy that more can be accomplished by working together. With mastermind groups, individuals motivated by a topic meet in an open, supportive environment usually once a week based on a set agenda with the purpose of sharing thoughts, ideas, opinions, and information that can help one another. I used this concept on a number of occasions for my own business and found it priceless.

Conduct a Mastermind Session

Ideally, each mastermind meeting should be conducted weekly or every other week, for one hour, in person, with all members of the group in attendance. Meetings can also be conducted over the phone. Each meeting follows a format such as the one I describe below for ensuring each member stays involved and gets their needs met. Your group should also assign someone to be the timekeeper–either the same person each session or rotating the task amongst the participants. The timekeeper ensures each portion of the meeting gets its allotted time and ensures that all members adhere to their pre-approved time to speak. We recommend that for the first few meetings, each member get the entire hour to familiarize the others with their situation, needs, and challenges, while the other members brainstorm ways they can support that person.

During later meetings, participants each get a small amount of time to update the others, ask for help, and get feedback.

What kind of discussions can you expect during a mastermind meeting? Here's an example that some of my clients have come up with:

- I need to up my skills level and perspectives for leading people
- I need innovative tools or ideas
- I'm lost at this new aspect of my leadership
- I'm looking for an expert to help me develop this idea
- Accountability through empowerment

In my work with leaders and employees, I've found the need to ensure alignment with understanding empowerment and accountability in the context of achieving high engagement for achieving results they can all be proud of. I start with collaborating with them to define what empowerment and accountability means to them. Here's what the general consensus was from various clients. Empowerment is the process of enabling or authorizing an individual to think, behave, take action, and influence work and decision making in autonomous ways. It is the state of feeling self-empowered to take control of one's own destiny. Accountability is doing the right thing consistently, day in and day out, in tasks and relationship interactions to fulfill or further the mission of the organization.

Focus on and commit to results, not excuses (e.g., blame, complain, no time). This involves you modelling focus and commitment to results, to coaching them from the inside-out. To align, make sure your team and cross-team roles are clear (not just generic job descriptions and standard operating procedures), that everyone knows what they're accountable for, that there are clear cross-boundaries, and licenses to create and innovate for everyone. Tap into their passion, talents/core genius, purpose as aligned with the organization's purpose, mission, vision, values.

Chapter 7:

TRANSFORMING FOR SUCCESS

"Greatness on the outside, begins within"
– Robin Sharma

ransforming for success does not just happen by simply following steps. It requires your efforts to discover your true self, and a fundamental part of that includes discovering what success means to you and how you make success last in everything you aspire to achieve. It also requires your unrelenting love (and its loving feelings of connection and joy) for what you discover about yourself, your brilliant possibilities, and what you choose to want and to do (to act on) from there. With this unrelenting love, it requires ongoing care and nurturing, which involves understanding ways for effectively removing self-defeating beliefs, fears, and habits that hold you back from achieving success.

When I started this journey of mine to write this book, my first book, part of my research for shaping what I wanted to say in these pages was finding a perfect definition of success. By perfect I mean that I wanted just the right definition to put context to my purposeful message: that success starts from within through love, and then out, not originating from an external place. I also wanted it to hit home that when internally-driven, success permeates from within which, in turn, expresses out to the external in a true and lasting way, extending beyond your individual success, to success for others. That's my definition of success for this book. Here's a definition of success which I found on the Ted Talks page and relates well with my context. It said, "Success can mean feeling that tingle of excitement about what you do, sticking with what matters through hard times, living a life you can feel proud of in retrospect." I love this definition because it qualifies that a strong positive force which evokes positive emotions is involved, that perseverance, commitment, and a feeling of self-fulfillment are required to reach success. That positive force is love. And so, if success starts from within through love, and then out – not the other way around – it would make sense that transforming for success starts with your inner transformation, incubating your power to express success out to your various life environments.

Transforming for success takes ongoing effort and nurturing so that your thoughts, beliefs, emotions, feelings, and actions/habits align and stick to success which is rooted on love. When success is rooted on love, your priorities and relationships are anchored to the values you hold – values that will align with achieving success. And yes, it takes work and ongoing efforts to ensure that your efforts are on par to seize whatever it takes to get you there. For the inner work, it also involves understanding how and what it takes for you, removing limiting beliefs, managing emotions, and releasing negative feelings that can lead you to self-defeat, fears, and habits that hold you back from transforming for success and are also harmful to your wellbeing.

Priorities Aligned to Values

Setting priorities that align with your values helps to keep you on track in your transformative journey for success. To align, these priorities are set on the values you hold (those things which you hold important and of worth) for your mind, soul/spirit (heart), and body.

When you value your mind, you will align your priorities with learning and gaining knowledge, taking time for a book or daily personal reflection to train your mind to work with you and not against you. There will be times when reframing your mind, to shifting your mindset is needed to align with what it will take within you to achieve what you set out to achieve.

When you value your soul (heart and spirit) you will align your priorities to help evolve your emotionality and feelings toward your life aspects, your faith and your beliefs that hold you to fulfilling what you are striving for with loving purpose and meaning. You will free your soul from limitations the ego puts on it, and create positive, "feel-good" experiences, staying in tune with your level of authenticity, and true purpose, in the context of love, joy and connection.

When you value your body, you will align your priorities to nourish and take care of it as best you can (which is more than just a whimsical attempt, but rather it is a regular routine). You will want to transform your body to keep it healthy by choosing to take care of it and to pay attention to what it needs.

Taking Care of Your Transformation

Transforming yourself for success is one of the most difficult and one of the greatest things you can do. It's a path of perseverance, patience, discipline, great challenge, and catharsis. It's also a path of meaningful discovery of yourself that brings you a renewed sense of capability and connection to your authentic self, to your authentic success in every area of your life. If you are willing to whole-heartedly seize your transformative path – and face the personal beasts that you'll meet there – then you'll transform yourself in a profound and brilliant way. The rewards for that effort and dedication are innumerable, significant and permeate from within to your external world. Learning how to achieve external success is comparatively easy. It is much harder to learn how to be aware, introspective, and understanding of who you are, how you show up in your life for self and others so that you can lead with meaning and lasting success.

Caring for Your Mind

Inner work is about your mind and making sure you take care of it. It's about ensuring a mindset that is aligned with what you set out with deliberation for achieving your goals – a mindset conditioned so that you're prepared for effectively facing and effectively responding to challenges and opportunities within your life environments. Transforming yourself and embracing the habits of inner, authentic success requires ongoing care because you will be tested with challenges along the way. It involves taking care of your inner attitude of your mind to align with achieving success. Ask yourself, how ready are you to meet the challenge? The path to success starts with what you invest in yourself. It starts with one day, today, always.

Chapter 4 touched on the importance of your mindset as the foundation for success and supporting you through your life environments, and in what you set out to achieve as a leader. The quality of your mind determines the quality of your life. If your thinking is unclear, clouded, filled with negative perspectives, and random, your results will reflect that, and others will be influenced by that too. If your mind is sharp, focused, clear, and capable of deliberate thoughts that attract the success you want, your results will reflect that, and others will be influenced by that too. If you value and care about leading a life you want, a highly engaged team that produces results, then care about cultivating a mind aligns with that value and care. It is in your mindset foundation that can achieve you the lasting success you are after.

Release the "Woe Is Me" Club and Embrace the Company of Success

Jim Rohn, the late, well known motivational speaker, self-made millionaire, and author of several best-seller books such as The Philosophy for Successful Living, once said "You are the average of the five people you spend the most time with." Our mindset standards are heavily influenced by who we associate with. If your primary social and professional circles have low standards for mindset development, this will surely affect your progress for transformation. Until you reach the point in your personal transformation where you are confident you no longer allow others to affect you with their negativity, its important to avoid people who bring you down or are not supportive (some call this "toxic" relationships). Think about those relationships you have that may be toxic to your mindset transformation for success and avoid them. If it's impossible (even though, I remind you, nothing is impossible; it is always a choice), severely decrease the amount of time you spend with them, or disengage in fostering conversation with them that keeps you stuck in whatever negative topic they are trying to engage you in. It's important to free yourself from the negative influence of others. You'll know you're in the company of people who are toxic to your transformation when you hear them always complaining and blaming others for their circumstances. Or those who are always critiquing others, gossiping, or talking about how bad their situation is in life. There may also be those you keep in company with that tend to regularly shoot down your dreams and aspirations or ideas, trying to dissuade you from believing in and pursuing your goals. If you start to get this feeling that you have people in your life who constantly try to bring you back down to their negative level – and this feeling is natural when you are going through a transformation journey – take it as a signal for you to avoid them or the situation unless you feel you can influence.

I once ran a two-day session with a group of leaders to teach a workplace success framework. As I mingled with them during lunch break, I had asked each person if they knew who the top three leaders were in their company. They had no problem telling me who these three were. When the workshop resumed, I then asked the group if they knew what these top three leaders' secrets of success were. It was amazing how no one had an answer, how this group knew who the most effective leaders were in their company, and yet, none of them had ever asked these top leaders to share their secrets. Perhaps not knowing was from a fear of being rejected if they did ask for the secrets.

To nurture your journey to reach success, you must start surrounding yourself with people who are successful in the area you're striving to succeed in – and ask. You must surround yourself with those who fill your life with bright, clear-minded people constantly learning, growing, improving their minds, demonstrating the habits you are cultivating for yourself, and have lessons and wisdoms they can share with you.

Move towards and embrace people who challenge you in a forward-moving way, who inspire you and who can be a constant presence in your life to remind you against wallowing in a mindset wasteland.

Complete Your Past

A major reason why some find it difficult to move forward in life is because they haven't properly dealt with the things that are holding them back. Many bind their mindset to anchors of past hurts, past anger or fear, past situations where closure has not happened at deep level – a past I refer to as incomplete. Releasing these anchors could be a liberating final step to complete your past and embrace your present which looks forward to your future. What replaces these anchors, are anchors born from love, connection, joy.

I've known people who have forgiven their significant relationship such as a spouse, or parents, and accelerated their life's productivity and ability to achieve their goals. I've also known others who have finally tackled and put in order their finances and doubled their income soon after as a result. I spent the weekend cleaning out my upstairs closets and bedrooms from old clothing and years' worth of unopened boxes – and scored a new client the following Monday. Complete your past so that you can focus on the present and shaping your future.

Try this. Take some time before the end of a month in this year and make a list of all the anchors that are weighing you down – those anchors from unresolved issues with family, loved ones, conversations, or decisions you've been putting off, house projects you've keep delaying. Take that list and create a schedule for completing each item on this list on a set date in that month you choose to target your completion. Mix up that list with easy completions and then build to the ones that may stretch you. This exercise will help to nurture your practice of completing incomplete things in your life. When you do this, I promise, you will be amazed at how liberating it feels.

Honour Your Successes

For many, there is a tendency to more easily remember their own failures, than remember their successes. Experts tell us that often we've been conditioned to recall our failures more so because of how we've been parented, taught, and managed in our childhood years. Perhaps you easily recall that moment you were scolded or paid more attention to for misbehaving, or that moment when you received attention because of your parents' worry for you having a failing mark in school. If you're a parent, you may also see how quick it is to pay more attention to your misbehaving teen, than when they are succeeding in school.

We tend to more easily remember events that bring about strong raw emotions, and when we fail at something, thinking about what that failure can bring about strong emotions that are negative. This in turn dilutes attention to acknowledging and appreciating actual successes that have been achieved – we get stuck in the negative feelings and lose sight of moving forward from a place that breeds success. As a result, we can resign ourselves to a reality that success, or the hope for it, is futile. However, when we can fully acknowledge our positive past (successes we've achieved), we can reinforce the positive emotions needed for the self-esteem and confident level building that's needed in transforming for success. We can release and replace the negative feelings and emotions by shifting our mindset to remembering success.

One of the exercises I do with my clients, which I learned during my success principles certification training, is to have them share one success they've achieved in the past week. It's surprising to see how difficult this is for many people. When going through this exercise, I've had clients who don't think they have had any successes. What they can recall, though, is a handful of things that they've not done well in, some even going as far as saying they are complete failures. To help my clients navigate through this discovery (once we have gone through it and I highlight their difficulty with identifying successes), I have them go through an exercise of making a list of major or significant successes from their life timeline, taking their current age, and dividing it by three equal time periods. For instance, a client of mine, Alice, is fifty. On her worksheet, she would have a list of successes for the first-third of her life from as far back as she can remember from the age period of 1-16 years; and then the second-third of her life which is age period from 17-32; then, age period from 33-50. This exercise helps to recondition your mindset to opening up to recognize successes you've had in the past, which boosts your self-esteem and confidence. I have found that when your self-esteem and confidence are high, you'll find that failures don't break or destroy you or your day.

Feed Your Mind with Quality Input

When I came back from an intensive ten-day transformation retreat – the kind where you were silent for five straight days, journaled daily, and walked on fire by then end of the session – the lowest volume of music on a radio would sound like it was on maximum dial. The mind is trained by sensory input. When the sensory inputs of television, internet, and social media were taken away from my head space for those retreat days, it was incredible how re-sensitized I felt. The incredible part of it was that I came back feeling heart-centred, my senses fully acute. Experts tell us that a high level of television watching, internet surfing, or social media gives your mind low-quality input and de-sensitizes you from the information you feed your mind. Take, for instance, the graphic video games kids comfortably play nowadays compared to the less graphic ones us mid-agers used to play.

Consider giving your mind a break from the information overload of all forms of electronics and focus on feeding your mind with high quality input such as reading books or attending informational sessions that are interactive. Take notes on what you read, what you hear in the seminars or workshops. Participate in absorbing the information. Seek to apply what you learn, so you can test the ideas for yourself. Another form of mind break is getting out in nature – go for a walk or run on a trail and absorb the beauty around you. Another great mind break is immersing yourself in something pleasurable that can take your mind off of your regular mind routine – go to that trampoline gym with your kids; laugh with your friends; take time to yourself and enjoy some silence.

Dive into the Deep End

With the abundance of information readily available and accessible on the internet, it's easy to bounce around from one topic to another and feel you're learning some worthwhile ideas. Often, however, this constant bouncing around limits the mind from digesting the information at a deep level. Learning experiences from this form of access can be shallow. To produce strong transformation effects that benefit your mind conditioning, consider a deeper dive learning, by attending experiential, interactive transformation coaching, workshops, and sessions, such as a 30-Day trial-challenge session. This is a great way to give your mind a taste of new experiences, get experiential guidance on time-tested insights and tools, try new habits (for longer than a day!), so you can make informed choices about your next steps in your transformation journey. Whatever the choice, make sure you choose to continue to nurture your transformation for success – deep dive into that nurturing and take care of your transformation.

Chapter 8:

STEP OUT OF THE COMFORT ZONE

"As you move outside of your comfort zone, what was once the unknown and frightening becomes your new normal."
– Robin Sharma

W e all know what it feels like to be in the comfort zone and likely we settle in it nicely like that blanket Linus (friend of Charlie Brown) carries around.

Whenever we venture outside our comfort zone, it can feel uncomfortable and for many, it's outright scary. In life, I've learned that fear comes knocking on our proverbial door whether imagined or actual when you do things you've never done or you're taking a risk. All sorts of doubts can creep their way into your mind and stop you in your tracks toward reaching your goal. That's why getting a handle on those doubts and fears are so essential to your success, an essential part of personal transformation work and mindset foundation building. I predict, from firsthand experience and witnessing of others, that as soon as you get a handle on those doubts and fears, you will be ready to create abundance in all areas of your life and help others that you lead.

When I work with my clients, I have them go through an experiential exercise to demonstrate the effects of imagined fear on reaching goals. I have them close their eyes and imagine they're on a small landing (just enough to stand on at full spread) on the top of a skyscraper (their choice such as CN Tower, Eiffel Towel, Empire State Building, etc.). The exercise helps them to confirm for themselves that it's not being at the top of the skyscraper that's frightening. It's the image/thought of falling off (a catastrophic event) that's frightening – yes, even though it's not really happening. Your body just feels that image you've pictured in your head and then responds to that picture as real. That's imagined fear. Coincidentally, I learned that this imagined fear (of a looming catastrophe) is at the heart of many phobias like fear of the dark or flying. To help my clients see there is a way to break their imagined fear, I then guide them through the next part of this exercise which is the release of these catastrophic images, guiding them to replace these images with positive images such as having the capacity to fly and enjoy the view.

Here's the thing though, staying on the "sunny side of life" (those positive thoughts) isn't to say you don't work through your feelings. On the contrary, those feelings are real, your mind has imagined that fear as real, then it is real, and you need to acknowledge that. What you do with those feelings is the key. When you become aware that your fear is imagined and not actually existing in your physical reality then you can make a healthier choice for getting back on track toward what you want. Here's another thing about the technique of "staying on the sunny side". To make the technique work for you, know that it isn't about burying or ignoring what negative feelings are experiencing. It's like, when you've just lost your job – Great! That's an opportunity for you to explore your passions and purpose. Or, you find out your spouse cheated on you with your best friend. At least you now know who you can count on and who you can't. The truth is, there are times when life sucks, and admitting it, accepting your feelings are healthy and needed to guide you to your next step – responding in a way that does not leave you stuck. Denying these emotions only leads to experiencing deeper and more prolonged negative emotions that can lead to deeper issues such as emotional disfunction and mental health issues leading to potential physiological issues like panic attacks, heart attacks, autoimmune problems, all very real stuff. When we deny and bury these emotions under that "sunny-side" perspective, we are not helping ourselves, we are avoiding. Now what you do with your negative feelings and emotions for getting back on healthy track, that's a whole new realm for consideration, and has something important to do with your values. The key here is to process through a negative emotion, to express it in a healthy manner that's socially acceptable and aligns with your values (what you hold as a principle you live by).

The Prize Just Outside of Comfort

If you want real growth and progress, know they don't come from staying where you feel comfortable. For me, if I had stayed in my comfort zone – where I had a home life with the comfort of a dual income – I would've dismissed the signs that it was abusive on more levels than one. Instead, I chose to leave that comfort zone. And here I am in my own home with limitless possibilities for what I want, not what I don't want. Even still, many more comfort zones appeared, testing me on whether I should take a leap and seize the uncomfortable chance of putting myself out there with speaking in public, leaving a cushy client relationship when I knew I wanted to do more than push paper for the almighty dollar.

For growth and progress to happen outside of the comfort zone you must do things you've never done (if you did them you would already be at the level goal you're aspiring). Some leaders I've worked with have issues with getting out of their comfort zone, which keeps them where they are, despite their desire to level up. Their reasons for staying in their comfort zone is largely due to fear of risk and leaving the habits and routines they've gotten used to for years (in some cases these include what they believe has helped them to cope and keep them in their role status).

I believe there is this universal challenge line we all experience on the progress continuum, that tests us, moving as we make decisions and take action. Let's look at this. You're at the start line (call it, your current state), and you've set your goals and actions to get to the finish line (your desired end state), and you are faced with challenges along the way. Along that path are a bunch of actions you're taking, and then suddenly, you're hit with a circumstance or two (and they do happen) that challenge you. It feels uncomfortable. Sometimes this discomfort leads you to believe the risks are too high to proceed, or that there are obstacles in the way that compel you to de-value the possibility to proceed (such as someone to blame or an excuse you really believe is valid to stop you from plowing through). When you get to this point, you stop and consider your options. At this point, you have at least three options – you can:

- Stop and decide it's your new start line
- Decide to retreat back to your original starting line or somewhere behind that stop point just ahead of your original starting point
- Decide to break through it and continue.

Only you can decide what's right for you. Make sure you're aware of this, that you're making a choice, that you have it in your power to choose. Next, do what it takes to make sure you have a well-informed perspective of the pros and cons to these options before deciding whether you move forward or backward in this continuum. There is no right or wrong, unless you decide it as so. If you choose to retreat, you'll be back to either square one (where you started) or a bit further, presented with the possibility of having another go at it (hopefully with gained insights that prepare you this time around). If you choose to pause and learn from gained insights to move forward, you've progressed a bit. If you choose it's downright not worth it at all, you stop altogether, and know that by doing this, you've decided this progress path is done. The key is to keep moving forward if progress is what you want. Your path may very well need tweaking, and involve iterations so just make sure that's the direction you're moving in. That universal challenge line that moves with you is a test line to see how badly you want that progress to take you to your finish line. Another key point to this is that when you break through that challenge line, you move forward which means more challenges to get through. When you break through any testing line in this continuum, the "poopy-pants" factor shows up and adds to your challenge test line, especially when you're just about get to the finish line. I say, you're on the right track when you feel this "poopy-pants" coming on. Plow through!

I want to share with you something that just happened this morning as I was writing. While it's a really small thing, it alludes to so much more of the point I'm highlighting here. So, I grabbed my pen and note-book and started to write. Four words in, this bold ink of my favourite pen ran out of ink. Without thinking much of it, I grabbed another pen, kept writing, and again – the pen ran out of ink. At this point, I'm laughing to myself, but also feeling a bit frustrated because I had a deadline. What did I do at this point? Take it as a sign this information was not meant to come out? Get frustrated and give up on the whole thing? Blame myself for leaving so many of my pens without ink? Nope. I caught my frustration, with no judgment, and grabbed a third pen, and this time, was able to finish my paragraph thought on paper. I met my deadline, simple, easy and effortlessly. My goal and intention was so much bigger than the challenge; and because of this, I glided right through it. Here's the thing, a pen or two running out of ink is like a little challenge to overcome. But this works with much bigger intentions and far greater challenges too. Consider this as an analogy that anytime you are trying to accomplish a goal, create something, grow, transform, or bring positive change into your life, there will be challenges. There will be roadblocks and unforeseen circumstances. Pens will run out of ink, you will feel frustrated, the internet will be down, roads will be closed, your flight will be delayed, you will come across crabby people. You get the idea. None of these things are signs that you are on the wrong track. Your ego might want you to think so that you give up, stop in your tracks, stay the same or revert back into the very habits and patters your setting out to transform. However, these challenges, obstacles, road-blocks are an essential part of the growth and transformation process. They are opportunities on the path for you to claim your mastery! They prove you are committed to your goal. They enable you to respond in a new way and to move through whatever it takes to stay committed to your highest intentions and responding with love.

To make sure you don't find yourself plateauing and to keep your-self on the track, keep these things in mind. They're meant to help start getting you out of your comfort zone so that you can get uncomfortable and start moving forward:

Push yourself beyond your comfort zone – don't be afraid to step out of your comfort zone. Be aware, seek what you need to support you in order to progress forward on a path that works for you.

By stepping out of your comfort zone, you have an opportunity to stay in the driver's seat of creating the reality you want. You make the decisions and you reap the rewards. One reward is that your tolerance and due-diligence threshold increases for taking risks for the sake of progress. This strengthens your ability to handle obstacles more effec-tively (better resolution tactics, better decision-making, better actions taking, for the sake of achieving what you want).

View stepping out of your comfort zone as a challenge test line, not a zone that leaves you with no other option but to settle for comfort.

Learn from your experience to quicken your pace in your forward movement. It's ok if you decide to stop in your tracks, but make sure you've learned something from it, keep practicing stepping out of the comfort zone to strengthen your ability to step out when it serves your progress goal. In professional swim training, coaches say that it's ok to "die out" during training, but the focus is on building stamina for pace, so by taking a faster pace, professional swimmers increase their pace for the real race.

Be willing to try and do different things. Don't just think that there's only one way. Welcome feedback or suggestions from others and try them out if the source is credible (knows what they're talking about). You may not feel comfortable with their feedback or suggestions, but you never know how great these options could be for your progress unless you try them. Another thing, by doing different things, you're also giving yourself an opportunity to strengthen your flexibility and versatility which are other key attributes that will serve you well for facing challenges and new opportunities that require innovation or outside of the box thinking.

Don't be afraid to associate and be in the company of those people who are already at the level of leadership you're aspiring, or who have reached a similar goal you've set out to achieve for yourself. It's tempting to stay in the company of people who are in the same boat as you are because it may seem comforting. You won't get judged and you can commiserate. Step out of your comfort zone and face that fear head on, by meeting with those who've levelled up to where you want to be (e.g., seek out a mentor in them, or arrange a mastermind group). This will push you to look for opportunities to improve yourself.

Be open to change and try new ideas. It's easy to fall into resisting change and new ideas because they're different from what you're used to. It's a natural human reaction to want to defend our current ways from change, especially in situations where you feel change is being imposed on you, such as inheriting an additional responsibility in your leadership role. When you're open and willing to change and try new ideas, new responsibilities, it'll only get you to a better place.

If you're presented with a challenge this week, or if a struggle or lesson from your past re-emerges, know that you can respond in a new way, always. Remember that when you have decided to transform, your are not who you used to be because you are focused on the bigger picture of who you are now, and where you are headed.

And in this moment now, with love in your heart and light in your field, you can move through challenges as easily as grabbing that new pen, and continue writing.

Fearless Grit for Success

As you move forward in your journey from where you are to where you want to be, it's inevitable that you'll need to confront your doubts and fears. Doubts and fears are natural and are a good signal, a signal to decide whether you take action or not. For some, doubt and/or fear stops them from taking the necessary steps toward their goals and dreams. On the other hand, I've learned (and promote with my clients) that successful people:

Feel the doubt and fear, welcome them because of how they serve their purpose. They incorporate this awareness in their actions, and they don't let it keep them from doing what they set out to accomplish

Take the time to practice the habits to deal with those fears and doubts

Willingly take themselves out of their comfort zone and understand that doubt/fear is something to be acknowledged, experienced, addressed, and taken along for the ride

Have strategies for anticipating, facing doubt/fear and taking appropriate action anyway – whether to mitigate, adjust, or face it head on.

Chapter 9:

RELATIONSHIPS MATTER

"Therefore, dear Sir, love your solitude and try to sing out with the pain it causes you. For those who are near you are far away... and this shows that the space around you is beginning to grow vast.... be happy about your growth, in which of course you can't take anyone with you, and be gentle with those who stay behind; be confident and calm in front of them and don't torment them with your doubts and don't frighten them with your faith or joy, which they wouldn't be able to comprehend. Seek out some simple and true feeling of what you have in common with them, which doesn't necessarily have to alter when you yourself change again and again; when you see them, love life in a form that is not your own and be indulgent toward those who are growing old, who are afraid of the aloneness that you trust.... and don't expect any understanding; but believe in a love that is being stored up for you like an inheritance, and have faith that in this love there is a strength and a blessing so large that you can travel as far as you wish without having to step outside it."
– Rainer Maria Rilke, *Letters to a Young Poet*

n life, we all have one core need and that need is Love – to give it and to receive it. I believe that love is the greatest energy force inherent in life that moves life's progress, creation, renewal, and healing. I believe that, from love, we achieve lasting success in everything that truly matters. We always have love in us, and depending on our choices, we can harness it for amazing results, or not. Oftentimes, we find ourselves mistaking love for feelings or acts of hurt, anger, withdrawal, competition, retribution, anxiety, fear of loss or giving too much than what others give to us. When we make this mistake, it's often subconscious, and we find ourselves far removed from the essence of love, basing our interactions with self and others, not from a place of love, but rather, from a place that limits the achievement of love which is the source for the results we are truly after. Take for example, the human potential in love-making. When we make love, we have the potential to create another human being that we have unconditional love for. Even if we are not able to procreate (as in cases of infertility), we have the potential to decide to adopt or go through medical procedures such as insemination or invitro, or surrogacy – for the sake of love. Regardless of procedure, when we decide we want to have and raise a baby or child, it is from pure love. Creating all other magnificent results for the world is the same.

At the heart of everything in our life, regardless of environment in which we operate, the channel for love (giving and receiving it) is through connection and relationships. We can either shut that channel off (thus, shutting off love), or we can open it to fill our relationships with love to unfold more openings for the flow of all good that love provides, including success results that matter for those involved, and even go beyond. In the natural, universal law of giving, it's through relationships that give us an opportunity to give and receive love – and love is the law of healthy relationships that expand the realization of thorough and lasting success. You must first relate with yourself through love, and then take that love to relate in this world, in your life.

True success, true progress, in anything, requires the ability to build and nurture connections and relationships that matter for who you are, for the kind of leader you want to be for self and others, and for the goals of each of the environments you influence because you have chosen to operate in them. Building and nurturing relationships that matter requires a fundamental understanding for the purpose of relationships, and that purpose is to give and receive love, to progress life, not stint or regress it.

Engagement Comes from Relationships

If you look at your relationships right now, you'll be able to gauge what you've been giving, by what you're receiving from them. In Chapter Four, I covered the relevance of thoughts and energy vibrations necessary for expanding what you focus on. Do you know what kind of vibration you're putting out in your life, in your relationships? I'm not just talking about right now. I'm talking about all the time. When you're just walking around, or cleaning your house, or paying bills, or at the office, at home with your family, or at a social with your friends – what kind of vibration are you sending out? The reason I'm asking is that it's easy to raise your energy vibration when you're thinking about it. And raising your vibration is essential for the frequency to attract what you're thinking about. When you're meditating, or praying, or visualizing for example, it's natural that your vibration would elevate to match your higher thoughts – those thoughts that are aligned to what you want, not what you don't want. But what about when you're tired or feeling frazzled? What about when things aren't going your way? What kind of vibration are you putting out then? There's a deep (and very distinct) connection between you and the world in which you live and operate (some refer to it as the Universe), and your vibration determines what you bring about (or some would call it, "manifest"). This means that if you're feeling tired and frazzled more than you're feeling connected and focused, you may not be creating the reality you want. And, that connection works both ways. So, just as the energy you sent out influences your reality, you can also use the world (universal) energy to influence you from within. This universal energy has incredible healing power and together with your thoughts and feelings, you can use it to raise your own energy aligned to the results you truly want. You can use it to clear out mental and emotional blocks, restore balance, even rejuvenate your entire energy system from the inside out.

I'm sure you know what it feels like to be in a good relationship, bad relationship, horrid relationship, annoying relationship, great relationship, or a relationship you learned from. Relationships are important to us for many reasons. The single, most important reason we must always consciously remember is that relationships are our biggest means to give and receive love. Through the love you give and receive in your connections and relationships, you are able to transform your life, your life's moments and results, to the love for the results you want to receive. I know this from first-hand experience and have numerous examples of how, through my own relationships in work, in family, in friendships, in serving others, the force of love has shown me that when love is given, it is received in spades – and it expands to spread out the magnificence of love's power to give every person in this love, brilliant growth and results that matter. So, in the spirit of what I mentioned earlier – that what you focus on expands – focus on love and channel it through the right relationships, and watch the energetic magic begin.

This chapter is profoundly important to me because I believe that at the heart of true success, you must love – and to love, you must first relate with yourself, in love, and then take that love to the world. At the heart of everything in our life, regardless of the environment in which we operate, the channel for love (giving and receiving) is relationships, which starts with you – the quality in relationships you choose to have, to give and receive. We can either shut that channel off (thus, shutting off love) or we can open it to fill our relationships with love to unfold more openings for the flow of all good that love provides, including success results that matter for all involved. It's our relationships that give us an opportunity to give and receive love – and love is the law of relationships.

Your "Why" for Right Relationships

In my own personal work and my work with clients, what I've come to realize is that the importance of relationships is often for reasons that keep us from our true purpose. We hold onto relationships that are not necessarily good for us; but rather, they keep us stuck in our limiting beliefs, our fixed mindset, rather than the growth mindset which promotes greater possibilities for positive results in our outcomes – a promotion of authentic and lasting success growth rooted from love, joy, connection, and harmony. There are fundamentals we all share as to why relationships are important, and I want to highlight them for you as a reminder, as an 'aha' for you and your next steps to choosing what you want to do when it comes to your relationships, as a leader.

For me, love is about the "why" that gives reason to what you do to create and relate in life. I wasn't always this clear with my purpose in life. In fact, I remember feeling so lost in a bunch of doing and being for others that I didn't even know who I was, let alone my purpose in life. It was like I was this empty shell and the only way I could find purpose was to fulfill someone else's needs. So, I figured if I could keep myself busy enough, it would hurt less. The opposite happened. I found myself in a state where I wasn't useful for someone else's needs. I was hurt from loneliness, depression, and unspeakable fatigue with life. I took relationships that were half fulfilling, meeting my half-Mr. Rights, thinking I could fix them. I immersed myself in jobs that would consume me, just to soothe my less-than-worthy self. I reached a breaking point, a breakdown that turned my life around for the positive, and out of the dark tunnel of self-loathing. I began to connect the dots of my purpose. I signed up for a personal transformation program in 2003 through the Hoffman Canada Institute and it was through the Hoffman

Process that led me to my clear path toward self-healing and claiming back power over my life. Over the course of the years that followed, I dedicated myself to more personal transformation work and I acquired tools that have helped me profoundly to be more present and include love in everything I do and everything I am. There is an exercise I go through with my clients from these personal learning experiences that helps them find clarity of purpose.

Why is finding your "why" in life so important? Living in your purpose feels alive, clear, and authentic. It allows you to experience that natural "flow," the state of total absorption when time seems to just disappear, and you feel so content and fulfilled. Your purpose guides and holds you accountable to attaining and nurturing the kind of relationships you want to attract. It offers emotional and psychological benefits which helps your physiological health. Having to manage my SLE Lupus, Sogrens' Disease, and Primary Biliary Cirrhosis, I can vouch for its health benefits. It also leads to healthier relationships and engagements in quality time with others.

I've experienced the healing power and force of love that produces my source of energy for everything I think, believe, feel, say, and do. In my self-work, I've processed through my relationships with self, others, and the environments in which I operate. I know how and what it takes to balance the relationships that are important to me, including the one with myself, and when I need to re-center, my commitment to ongoing transformation is there.

When working with my clients, I cover relationships and healthy choices, stressing that everything starts with a healthy relationship with self.

You are a whole being, and when you don't feel whole, it's because parts of your whole self are fragmented to fit to each of the demands of the external systems at play in your life – not just work, not just family, not just social; but all of them at the same time. In this fragmentation, often we make choices to sacrifice ourselves to feelings of obligation to others, and we bury our authentic feeling for self-love to meet the needs of others. What I have found is that such a relationship choice only causes more distance from love and a closer relationship to resentment, guilt, depression, hatred – not love. Serving others from a place of self-love is not about feeling an obligation that builds resentment, or an expectation of pay-back, or sacrifice of true self.

So where do you begin when it comes to understanding and caring for your relationships? Your relationship with self-acts as the base for what you achieve in your life, good or bad – and if you focus on yourself and work through this with your purpose, you'll attract the relationships you want.

We Grow, Relationships Grow

The following are the key elements that I cover and guide my clients through, for growing the right relationships that stick to authentic success and which are rooted in the concept of wholistic relationships that matter with the goal of connecting in the context of love and joy:

- Choices, challenges, and lessons
- Relationship with self – within the seven aspects of life that generally matter to individuals (personal, body/health, relationships, business/career, financial, community/legacy)
- Relationship with environment
- Relationships with others
- Healthy relationships with others
- Associations that support
- Relationships goal-setting

Choices as Relates to Challenges and Lessons

Challenges in relationships occur, that's a fact. It makes sense when you think of it. You have two people who have their own thoughts, beliefs, preferences, perspectives, principles way of doing things and wants that are not always going to be in line with yours. You have team members, family members, friends, romantic partners, social networks, colleagues, your one-up leader, your neighbours, and so on. Yes, it's a fact that challenges between you and those you relate with will come up. Learning to accept and welcome certain challenges of difference and working them out for the sake of a common goal will be required. Words and their tone, behaviour/attitude, body language, and actions are powerful and can destroy or nurture relationships. You have the right to choose the relationships you want to have and whether or not to nurture, stay, or walk away. If you want to be in, and surround yourself with, healthy, engaging relationships that produce aligned stellar results, then focus on that and the limitless positive possibilities you can create to acquiring it.

Remind yourself that challenges are inevitable, and they are also gifts for you to become aware of what it is you can learn and improve on in your relationships, starting with yourself. You cannot control events from happening, but you can control how you respond to them, in the moment and for the sake of the future you want. Easier said than done, I know. Your negative inner voice will creep in and try to convince you that you're a magnet for jerks that walk all over you; or maybe that you don't have what it takes to keep and have healthy relationships. If you believe that, it will become reality. Choose what you want to believe and be conscious about committing to that choice. When you introspect, you'll find the answer to your solution path to getting things back on track lie within you, waiting for you to connect to it, and make it a reality – this is why self-relationship is critical to base all other relationships.

We hear so much about relationships – relationships of partnerships, friendships, family relationships, work relationships and even those relationships that have ended. To me, these are external-based relationships and while important in their own right for us, our focus on them tends to outweigh the single most important relationship of them all – the relationship with self.

One of my favourite fiction books (and I don't have many) is Robin Sharma's The Monk Who Sold His Ferrari, which, in many ways, was a significant contributor to changing my perspective on how I lead my own life and relationships. If you haven't read it, do – it's a quick, easy, and enjoyable read. I loved it for those reasons and for the message it expressed: that all success comes from within, so prioritize caring for the relationship with yourself. Basically, the book is about a corporate lawyer who lost himself to his external relationships (work, people), and through a near-death experience (heart attack) finds himself going through an inner journey, described in magnificent and exotic (to me) detail, that brings him back to connecting with himself after recovering from his heart attack and leaving his law practice (yes, also selling his Ferrari and material possessions). The book hit home with its message about taking time to care for your self-relationship for true success.

I've learned personally that, in order to care for your self-relationship you need to self-actualize. Through self-actualization, we can choose where to place our awareness of who we are. Coined by organismic theorist Kurt Goldstein (and carried further by Maslow's theory of our basic and meta (hierarchical needs for our sense of belonging and progressive outputs in our life), self-actualization is basically a process whereby an individual realizes their true self-potential and self-fulfillment. We spend the better part of our lives focusing on our relationships with others (which includes comparing ourselves to them) that we tend to bury our own true essence. Our true essence (the "I" which experts in the field of psychology call the "highest self") is where we express our brilliance in life and to the world.

From self-actualization, you're able to obtain insights for an effective roadmap for self-care and self-relationship. In the Factor framework, the process of self-actualization is initially introduced in the Framing for Focus phase and iteratively throughout the other phases since each Factor phase pulls from elements of success habits teachings, depending on where one is in their journey.

Surrounding this "highest self" are six psychological functions (intellect, emotions, imagination, intuition, body, will), all of which are factors for fulfilling your goals, aspirations, and authentic success. The key is balance across each of these functions. Tools and techniques such as mediation for awareness and self-affirmation exercises are useful for this process towards balancing (e.g., visualization of purpose and goals; guided journaling for positive reframing statements; emotional freedom technique also known as "tapping" and the Sedona Method for releasing negative emotions and non-clinical tensions such as breathing regulation; muscle-testing for decision-making).

Through self-actualization, you're able to unlock your ability to choose which of these functions needs to be cared for if out of balance. Balance is key to a healthy relationship with the highest self – which, in turn, creates healthy relationships with others and the environments in which you operate in your life.

Each of the psychological functions that surround our highest self requires tools and techniques that can help you strengthen your balance across them, which I cover extensively with my clients. The curriculum I cover includes:

Intellect

Intellect is our mind's capacity and power to think, acquire knowledge, and understand. It's critical for shaping our thoughts, beliefs, and supporting actions that serve our purpose. Ensuring our mind's capacity and power requires the ability to align with what we want to achieve, rather than what we don't want. This involves processing, releasing, and replacing negative self-talk with positive self-talk and affirmations to support this. For instance, I recall a client of mine, Johnathan, regularly using life-impacting statements that often hindered him from achieving the success he wanted and deserved, and he didn't even realize it until I brought it up to him. He regularly used statements like, "I'm so bad with remembering names," "I am not good with people." "I always have issues, I'm not very lucky." What he soon realized after my first session with him was that such statements dictated what was showing up in his life – more of what he did not want.

Enhancing self-concept to align with the right beliefs is also important within your intellect. Knowing your true self through leveraging self-awareness, reflection, actualization, and introspection are critical to enhancing self-concept with the right techniques to support transformative success (techniques such as meditation and practicing success habits).

Imagination

Utilize your ability to creatively imagine the end state you want and feel the feelings associated with loving and being joyful about that end state. Know that if that imagination does not make you feel joyful and loving, it's your intuition telling you that it's not the end state you want. You should quickly get out of that state. Here, I encourage my clients to create positive mental images, often using visualization techniques such as vision boarding and journaling. This helps you to create a mental picture of your ideal state with the most positive feelings.

It's important for you to use positive mental images to access your inner wisdom for what you want. This enables you access a resourceful state of mind, to accelerate learning, and increase your memory for recalling positive thoughts associated with all that goes into your desired end state (what you want to achieve). Imagining from the most positive state allows you to also let go of all limiting beliefs and judgements. It creates a necessary structural tension inherent in all effective creative processes that reduces the effect of ego, increases resourcefulness (even synergistic collaboration) and more quickly leads to better plans for achievement of the right things. Imagine freely and creatively what you want, without worrying about the "how" you will achieve it –see what amazing mental images you come up with, and lock yourself into the positive emotions you get from your visualization of what you want to achieve, as though you've already achieved it.

When using your imagination, know that past recall can bring up negative experiences that may show up in your current moment which causes you to imagine the worst (hence, for instance, why Johnathan uses the excuse statement that issues always come his way and that he's not very lucky). When you use imagination to recall a negative experience, your imagination is not serving your alignment to your success goal. Healing the past is a big part of the inner work, making sure you identify the healthy supports you'll need for the processing of past hurts you uncover in this healing process (e.g., therapy counselling, a personal coach).

Emotional

Emotions are affective states of consciousness which are often accompanied by physiological effects such as joy, sorry, fear, hate. They are natural and inherent within every human being. Often, I've found that many deny themselves of emotions or let their emotions run amok when faced with a situation or circumstance. Accepting and managing our emotions, through the values we hold dear, in the spirit of love, joy, harmony, and connection is important to enable the cognitive (knowledge, perception, judgement) and volitional (willingness and intentions) states of consciousness within our mindset. Learning to accept emotions and manage them for responses to outcomes is important to your alignment to any success you are trying to achieve. Processing and releasing negative feelings from emotions (e.g., resentment, guilt, doubt, anxiety, fear) and positive re-framing are key to ensure healthy emotional expression and alignment to your goals.

Ultimately, strengthening emotional intelligence, which is the emotional capacity for recognizing our own feelings and those of others, is the ideal for managing emotions in a way that serves your true purpose. Emotional intelligence helps in:

- Motivating ourselves
- Effectively managing emotions well in ourselves and in our relationships

- Effectively managing our own feelings (self-assessment), so that we can also
- Recognize feelings of others and coach
- Managing self and enhancing relationships

Intuition

Learning to nurture, access, and trust your intuition (your "gut" feeling) with intention and purpose that matches what you want, not what you don't want, is key to balance and keeping to your true purpose and finding authentic success. Listen to yourself, and trust your feelings.

Body

Connect your heart and mind with body for wholeness and healing (e.g., meeting your needs for touch and nurturance though hugs, massage, healing, intimacy). Using stress management and reduction techniques also help to energize and enhance engagement while keeping you balanced. Love and appreciate your body by caring and nurturing it with healthy choices and habits, not self-destructive habits such as binge/overeating, sleep deprivation, under-eating, abuse, addictions.

Will

With the will to take action, you can achieve what you want. One of the brilliant resources available always is choice. When choosing, you open the gate of opportunity to achieve what you want; but it takes the right willingness to take action to achieving it. In my approach with clients, I teach them success principles and habits that galvanizes the practice and demonstration of will:

- Taking full responsibility for outcomes in your life
- Learning to make healthy decisions and responsible choices
- Practicing and exercising self-discipline
- Increasing commitment through action, setting goals that stick to success and your purpose / acting with integrity

- Taking accountability / learning to manage consequences and successes
- Relationship from Self with External (Social and Environments)

In an organization, as I mentioned previously, your relationship with the organization comes with the roles you need to play and perform in that environment. Taking a look at your job/roles and balancing that relationship with your core highest self-relationship is essential so that you don't find yourself detaching from your healthy self-relationship. I've seen many people lose themselves to their organizational environment, and I also know it from first-hand experience. Working insane hours, gossiping with others, complaining, blaming, feeling burned out, sacrificing our time for family relationships, are some tell-tale signs that you are out of balance with your self-relationship. These habits are contrary to achieving success.

Engagement and Alignment in the Organization

In organizations, I've found that because employee engagement tools measure organizational factors only, individuals are not given an opportunity to reflect and evaluate how other factors in their personal life affect their workplace engagement. It's a missed engagement source opportunity when organizations leave out considering their employees' personal engagement needs. Personal transformation sessions for both leaders and employees could help in dealing with the challenge of productivity through employee engagement. What I've found in my experience with organizations is that the standard personal supports available for their people is an Employee Assistance Program and coaching from their managers, who, by the way, would benefit from personal transformation work also.

Build the Right Relationships

To build the right relationships, I've come to realize that there are minimum skills and attributes, all based on a mindset that believes and is committed to creating successful relationships. Here's what I've learned. To create and build successful and engaging relationships for success, you must:

- Be present for yourself, and for others – master the art of listening
- Speak with love, intention, honesty, integrity, and engage from the heart
- Be lovingly honest, without hesitation
- If you find yourself doubting a relationship, step up: ask, clarify, recalibrate
- Truly appreciate the good and the bad
- Show commitment – hold to your agreements
- Offer the kind of relationship you would want, always.

As a leader, your ability to ensure healthy and positive workplace relationships are essential to influencing aligned engagement and productivity for success realization across your team. Powerful words and actions can destroy or flourish engagement for success. I mentioned that relationships start with self-relationship, and then across the external relationships you have in your life. Your team also needs to realize this, and you have an opportunity to practice it, and model it for their own self-relationship journey.

Fun, experiential, and interactive team-building exercises to get to know one another, from team and personal profiles of personality traits, perspectives, preferences, joys, values, and needs can help to engage your team and enhance healthy relationships. I use my certification in True Colors® (from True Colors International) and others such DISC profiling to facilitate this with my clients.

Section III

Perspectives and Further Guidance for Continued Success

Chapter 10:
OBSTACLES

"One word frees us of all the weight and pain of life:
That word is love."
– Sophocles

The Key Is to Believe

've shared with you the key to how you can make a difference as a leader and turn things around for you and others, and it's my hope that my messages have confirmed the fact that it is through you that the limitless opportunities available to you can be released for your success path in making a real difference. It's not about solving a problem and getting back to the grind, so you can find yourself back to the "square one" that had you in angst in the first place (and time and again). It's about prioritizing the whole you and opening your mind, calming it for focus and the right energy through a belief that you can seize all that you love and find joy, passion, and purpose in – and from there, to respond to whatever comes your way with purpose and vigour that makes a differ-ence because you are centered. As you may have sensed, the FACTOR framework is deceptively simple, personally powerful and profound, maybe even ambiguous. It's an ongoing transformative and experiential way of being in your life environments that guides your frame of reference, so that you choose your path to achieve wholistic and authentic success, not solve a problem through a one-time prescription pill – it's a transformation, and the key is belief through you. It's not for the skeptic, nor the ones who wish to stay with common, nor the faint-hearted, nor those fixed in believing there's only one way to make things better. It's for you, the one who continually seeks for better, the one who is brave enough to see and seize what's on the other side of comfort. It's for the you that has always known that there is so much more to life than what's in front of us in this moment, from beneath the skin of ordinary.

When you anointed yourself as a leader, it came from you, from your heart and mind. Choose to continue to expand from that choice. The approach I've provided works to enable you to expand, gathering techniques and self-discoveries that will keep you centred and focused on your heart-mind-intention goal. Choose to dive into this an approach that guides you to awaken to your being – a being that is clear, focused, not alone, nor lost, nor limited, nor confused, nor tired of, nor overwhelmed by life. You will know how to return to yourself and re-center, regardless of what comes your way in your life, because you know you, and you create in the context of love and joy, everything great that is possible for you and those around you in each present moment of your existence. You know you make a difference. The approach described between the covers of this book comes to life for you, when you accept it and make it come to life. By having read through the pages in this book, you'll see you've already started to open yourself to connecting with the leader in you that makes a difference. Before we complete our journey together in this, I want to offer a few more guideposts for you, just to make sure your beacon is brightly shining when the temptations for being thrown off course come knocking on your door as you continue in your own journey.

Challenges and Guarantees

Generally, in life, obstacles and challenges are inevitable and unpredictable, and how we experience them, how we respond to them, depends on our choices. In leadership, add to this the fact that inevitable and unpredictable obstacles and challenges will also be coming from at least three life environments that each have other principles, disciplines and processes that affect your choices and the choices of others you lead – the life environments of work, home, personal. The transformative framework I've offered can help guide you through these and your choices for addressing your success path to achieving your leadership goal to make a marked difference with your team, within this inevitable and unpredictable reality that challenges will always exist, but you're ready. There are no absolute guarantees when it comes to charting a fool-proof personal course for a better future. However, the fundamental principles and habits to success that I've shared with you throughout this book will go a long way to ensuring your professional and personal life will be immeasurably blessed. They've worked for me and are time-tested and proven by thousands of others. One simple shift that could change your outcomes, your life, forever – that's all it takes.

The Lurch and Sway of Change Exists

If something is made to be different from its original state, you have to change. To progress, change has to happen, no matter what. While that's all said and done, change is for the better or for the worse, depending on how you view it, prepare for it, handle it and learn from it. Most organizations experience waves of change, one on top of the other, on top of the other. And people in these organizations must make the transition from one reality to the next, over and over again. I've seen leaders and employees run at a high emotional pitch and its growing more and more – one wouldn't have to wait for an engagement survey to see it; just feel the atmosphere and for some, the results of status quo at best. From my experience, leaders recognize the need to manage business and provide effective leadership, but most often than not, it's the focus on the people side of leadership that tends to take second fiddle. While leaders may have mastered the structural side of leading: creating vision, change management, setting strategy, restructuring, and so on, structural challenges are exactly that, structural. This is all well for the structural challenges of organizational change. But what I've found often overlooked is the human side of change – what people need to let go, to build hope, to learn and to grow, wholistically. This requires leading people in a way that reflects their understanding, empathically recognizing the whole person and the many life environments at play when organizational change occurs. Leaders who minimize or ignore the powerful emotional undercurrents that accompany change and transition, risk the bottom line. Strategies (even great ones) and change initiatives stall or fail when employees are not committed and engaged, bottom line. Trust erodes, and what remains is a cultural atmosphere of apathy, fear, skepticism, unproductivity. Employees may be compliant, and just getting by, but they are not committed. Addressing this takes an inside-out transformative approach, starting with the leader and permeated out to each team member. Through this transformative framework, you will become a transformation leader because you will know that to make a difference with lasting results, it's all about everyone's thoughts and behavioural changes through transitions inherent in change, making the right decisions and acting from them through inevitable dilemmas, leading your goal for transforming to a highly engaged team that produces aligned results from authentic success in the context of love and joy. You will feel discomfort and pain but believe that when you embrace change and break through the discomfort, pain and all the gruel that comes with it, you will be for the better, you will model and coach from authenticity, you will prove your mark as a great leader, and you will get to the other side, which by the way, is where your desired future state is, remember. Choose and decide to become the best you can be, one day at a time, and see how it's from the best you where you'll find clear focus on resolving anything, achieving anything you set your mind and heart to.

Fear and Doubt Will Arrive for You

I covered this in Chapter 8, fears and doubts and this whole notion that there's this universal challenge test line that gets between where we are to where we want to be – achieve the success we want. Be ready, because these will arrive for you as you continue your transformative journey and path to achieving your goal. Fear, as natural as it is, is pretty scary, wouldn't you say? It causes us to doubt ourselves, to hesitate, even to stop us dead-cold in our tracks, and to lose faith in our capability to lead the life we were meant to live. Know that fear is a crucial response to danger (physical and emotional). It acts as our natural protection response from legitimate threats – back in the caveman days, those threats resulted in life-or-death consequences, such as starvation or hungry predators. Today though, we often fear situations with threats that are much lower in consequences than life-or-death, yet our mind and body still treat them as a threat. In today's modern world, we experience fear from impressions we'll make on others, relinquishing the destiny of our self-worth to someone else's judgement or approval of us. This can trigger an extreme and often-times unnecessary fight-flight-freeze-or-breakdown response from us. As a result, we find ourselves avoiding challenges that could actually benefit us in the long run. It doesn't help that our self-image is affected by what we see in social media and the internet readily bombarding us with an image we compare ourselves to, or our childhood programming that taught us to fear the unknown beyond the boundaries of should's and should not's. At times, there is a lingering trauma from experience that trigger our fear and doubt response within us that make it difficult to shake, even when there's no longer a risk warranting the fear or doubt in our capabilities. Consequently, most fears and doubts we experience are self-created by imagining some catastrophic event in the future – an event that hasn't actually happened but feels real to us because we hold this mental image in our mind which causes us to experience the fear in our body which cannot distinguish between a real event and an imagined one. Managing these types of fears and doubts in our abilities is challenging especially since they don't necessarily point to a clear and obvious danger. In the context of achieving our goals, when we allow our fears and doubts to take over us, despite the nil-margin for impending death or real risk, I have found that fear and doubt to be the biggest killers to achieving success. When we welcome fear and doubt to linger without managing it we can lose faith and trust in ourselves and we shrink from our right to be better, to achieve better, to creatively live, give and receive better in the context of love and joy, which is, well, fearless. Be aware that fear and doubt exist and will arrive, but you will be ready. Your life purpose comes from your mind and heart cohesion and becomes your internal global positioning system (G.P.S.) that will navigate you. This method sharpens your intuition, keeps you connected to your true source for achieving results from your alignment with your true passions and purpose in life, without fear of failure – no matter how deep that fear runs in your D.N.A. Your goal to make a true difference in the world is a larger force than the fear and doubt that will come for you. Why? Because your call to make a difference comes from the largest and most attractive force of them all, love. Stay your course, and you'll see this to be true.

You Will Feel Disconnected

On the one hand, you have your heart, which knows your inner truth. Your infinite potential to be and do great. On the other hand, you have your mind, which seeks to understand through logic and reason. When your heart believes one thing, but your mind believes another, you will only manifest more disconnect within yourself, and the limited results will be the outcome. But when your heart and mind are fully connected you create an intention that is purposeful and clear, in the context of love, and you'll be able to use your entire being as a magnet, designed to work everyone and everything in your life (not against it). Believe that it gets better each time you practice faith in that belief. Seeing is believing, and when anyone sees what they want as strongly as you do, they're halfway there when it comes to feeling abundant and whole, ready to seize their moments for great. Your imagination and creativity are critical for inspiring and engaging others. Your transformation journey will sharpen your ability to envision yourself manifesting your vision for what it is you want, with your heart and mind connected.

You know what could make you feel twice, three times, if not a million times, the power of your thoughts? The guiding framework offered in this book. Those who come to realize their personal power start to see the real results they've been searching for.

You Will Get You Stuck

Feeling stuck is the worst, isn't it? It's like you're walking around with a backpack full of rocks on your shoulders and slogging through life. You know why that happens? Because of a hidden little conflict inside that's pulling you in two directions at once (as I mentioned above)! I know what it's like to know what you have to do, but for some reason, you just can't seem to do it. It's like your body weighs a thousand pounds when you need to get up to present your compelling strategy everyone is waiting for. You feel frozen when you need to take action. Sometimes it doesn't even matter if you're conscious of what's blocking you or not because it feels so paralyzing you can hardly move.

Why do we get stuck? We generate fear, doubt, all the negative thoughts and emotions, and allow these to take over – and bam, what we focused on expanded into negative results that freeze any chance for achieving what we wanted. Through your journey, this will come up, but don't lose heart – use these moments as a reminder for you to feel your way through what you've learned in your journey. When we keep the connection of our mind and heart to our core purpose, we center our intention point to a razor-sharp focus on our intention/goal and bring about the results we want from this. You've learned that there are techniques (such as affirmations of positive thinking, re-framing from a place of gratitude, joy and purpose) to help you flush stress and anxiety out of your body like water down the drain. Know that you can keep calm and stay in control because you choose so, and you believe! You believe you have the tools to remove creative blockages so your mind and heart are aligned with your core self, clarity of purpose, passion, and intention, and these will erupt with startling new insights, allowing you to find solutions you could never see before.

You Will Stand Out and Sometimes Alone

"If right now our emotional reaction to seeing a certain person or hearing certain news is to fly into a rage or to get despondent or something equally extreme, it's because we have been cultivating that particular habit for a very long time."
– Pema Chodron, Tibetan Buddhist

Some people may get jealous or amplify their skepticism for your leadership because they are stuck in their old ways and habits. But know this, you'll attract those who've been waiting for someone that took a stand to consistently act from the wholistic self. For these people, they see an opportunity to awaken, as you did. What's inherent in a great leader are key characteristics that make them great. They have courage, tenacity, and patience, and belief in something greater than what exists today, for all. They have the courage to stand alone, the unwavering tenacity to stick it through (and break through) despite challenges and struggles; the patience to stay the course and guide others; and the demonstration of belief through commitment and accountability, until you win the day, which is every day.

You Will Want to Work Harder

I've come to realize in my years (both personal and professional) that many put themselves last, and other people first. I mean, self-sacrifice means you care, right? Well, no. We've felt too comfortable with associating self-sacrifice with "doing what's right." I don't believe this is how you achieve your goals or help others. Instead you build an endless "to do" list filled with other people's expectations, never living a life that truly matters to you! And guess what, you end up feeling badly when it's not paid back in kind or the results to your "sacrifice" are regrettably dismal. When we find ourselves in the state of thinking that if we work harder at the sacrifice of something important to us at core, we will reach our results. Yes we may very well achieve results, but we also create a pay-back and undermine sustainable success. When you come from the place of mind-heart intention, you find it isn't about working harder, it's about the inspirational effort that comes from each person's mind-heart intention to express love as a whole person, their belief that they will always achieve results because they act from feeling connected and being whole. It's important to understand and achieve authentic and lasting results from truly valuing the whole person as a human with core passions, purpose, and talents, not as a resource that can be moulded from external drivers. External drivers such as money, evaluative and material recognition are influencers, but they are secondary drivers. Go for the internal, the primary drivers of engagement. If you model from practice that you realize "Yes! I do deserve to get what I want authentically and in the context of love and joy!" you will create a force that attracts others to want the same for themselves. You will align the right alignment for engagement and achieving results from authentic success. The alignment that makes a true difference is engaging others from demonstrating that you will yourself, not others; and in turn, others will themselves. A simple shift in self-worth is all it takes to unleash the source of effective action. Because at the end of the day, what makes the biggest difference in your success is the action you take whole-heartedly, one day at a time.

Your Beliefs Will Be Tested

> *"Beliefs have the power to create and the power to destroy.*
> *Human beings have the awesome ability*
> *to take any experience of their lives and*
> *create a meaning that disempowers them*
> *or one that can literally save their lives."*
> – Tony Robbins

As you continue your transformation journey and start making positive momentum with realizing its wonders showing up in your life, you will also face others' beliefs in action along the way, that won't be aligned with your beliefs. Belief is formed when you develop a much larger base of reference, one that's often associated with strong emotions and based on experience. Beliefs can create such a level of certainty that they close people off to new ideas.

Expect that some may be stuck in their own beliefs, often those that have kept them in the state of disengagement they find themselves in. They hold to beliefs of defeat, that "all is lost, change will happen again and again so why bother…it's just a job and it pays the bills, so I'll keep my nose down, do what I'm told, and just work until I can find something better" mentality. These beliefs are limiting their potential to reach their greatest heights, and you will be tempted to join them in this belief, especially when it's more than one individual on your team that believe this. I mentioned in chapter 5 the power of thoughts, that it takes engaging others to make something you believe in come to life. Your disengaged team may not realize it (or maybe they do, covertly), but they are engaging others in disengagement by the demonstration of their belief that life at work sucks. What's equally concerning is that there may be some members of your team that don't share in their beliefs, yet because those limiting beliefs seem to be the only thing they experience around them, they get disheartened, keep quiet, and secretly wish for a miracle to help them through the energy-zapping drudge of getting through their work day. As a leader, you have the opportunity, through your transformation, to engage your team in your belief that, together, amazing results for all are possible and within your reach. When you demonstrate your belief, you're practicing faith in what you believe in, through your actions and by this you create a frequency for your belief, which attracts like-minds and hearts. The truth is, you demonstrate your belief when you show your commitment to that belief, through actions, despite whatever roadblocks and challenges appear. Life is often likened to a classroom, and yes, there are tests. These tests are opportunities to grow, to expand, evolve and respond in a new way.

Imagine this as Reality: You Are Unstoppable When You Have A Guide

You're meant to succeed and make a difference through your leadership! That's how you've succeeded in the past. Once you set yourself on accomplishing something, you'll always figure out a way to make it work! Where most people give up and submit to failure and problems, you keep the faith and stay the course, with authenticity. This is your spirit hungry for experience and living life to your fullest potential! You can do it alone, or you can accelerate your results in lesser time so that you can start engaging others, if you use a guide. The guide I offer in this book and through my coaching are based on proven principles and habits of authentic success that can take you from where you're at now, to where you want to go. Whatever you decide, make sure you stay focused on guiding ways that keep you from spinning your wheels with delusional positivity and getting nowhere fast.

Love's Sequence to Healing the World

The framework offered in this book is intended to guide you on your journey to authentic success and leading from that, to reach the greatest heights for what you seek today, and for what you seek that resonates for the tomorrows that follow. This is your leadership that makes a difference. That difference is that you understand to achieve lasting success, it comes from authentic success in the context of love for the whole self in you and in others. It starts with your authentic success and in the context of love, for you. It's through your transformation journey to this, your own healing and love for yourself that shows a path for others to follow. Every step you take in your transformation is an integral step that can make a difference for others in their process. Positive results will unfold each step of the way, because you feel the difference, you love this difference, and others are moved by this for themselves. As Goethe inspiringly states, "We are shaped and fashioned by those we love." Choose to demonstrate your love for your true self through your transformation journey, and model this for others in every aspect of your life. Love's journey is ongoing, and when taken, beauty unfolds every step of the way. You make a difference through your leadership, because you lead your whole life from love – and you model, inspire, and engage from this.

Chapter 11:

BEGINNING: THE WAY TO AUTHENTIC SUCCESS

"Try not to become a person of success,
but rather try to become a person of value."
– Albert Einstein

want to thank you here for the curiosity, openness, and courage to welcoming what you've learned through these pages. By doing so, we've reached a beginning, not a conclusion.

I believe that we're collectively building a sort of healing shelter within organizations where we can nurture one another and truly achieve lasting success by deliberate design and commitment to wholistic achievement – one that prioritizes the balance of progress with personal growth – both for the organization and for the whole person – in the context of love and joy.

I believe that the creative spirit in the name of love within each of us is the real antidote for our own and planetary healing from our current thinking and the substance behind everything that we are meant to be and achieve in life. When the noise and distraction of life's circumstances are pushed aside for a moment, I believe that we intuitively know this, and that this is how we as leaders can work together to reclaim our divine birthright and our right to guide and create a healthy future.

An organization comes to life because of its people – not bits and pieces of them. It's time to tap into this for brilliant results to show up for ourselves and for others.

As a leader, you have an incredible possibility before you to be that inspiring and healing tribal guide for your team, as they enter, live, express, and relate in your organizational world, bringing with them all that makes them special, as you are. When each of us strips ourselves of everything that consumes us, we will find our common ground that we have a heart, a soul, a mind, core talents, a body that makes the difference, because we are each a gift to the world waiting to fully express, in whatever it is we set out to achieve and progress. And it is in the context of love and joy, that such deliberation for results, that true success exponentially expands, grows, and is sustained. Continually coming from this brings about a remarkable frequency for a healed world where we think, believe, behave, and act on achieving success that serves all, because we heal, we give, we receive, and we progress in the name of love.

Imagine we are seated on the bank of a sparkling stream one evening. There is a warm breeze that gently soothes our skin and rustles the nearby leaves to add to our soothing sensations. We are comforted by the company and nature that surrounds us. Imagine we are speaking in subdued tones about the sacredness of our work and personal struggles. At work, we are bound as we all too often are, within rigid angles and lighting, uncommitted colors of the walls that surround us, encased within our cubicles, and we do not speak of such things as spirit, soul, joy, fear, despair, grief, loneliness, passion, love, priority other than work. Here, by this bank of sparkling stream, we speak of these things and all that make us feel we belong in the nurturing arms of our company, honouring the awareness we have for one another, that everyone experiences them, and that we are supported.

We speak of these things with the common understanding that they reverberate throughout the work environment, disturbing our sense of self, our souls, profoundly, knowing these things permeate across the workplace with whom we share the same space, meeting rooms, strategic plans, performance targets, deadlines, tasks, reports, and performance appraisals.

By this bank of sparkling stream, we speak of these sacred truths, and we feel afraid, weak, tired, and unworthy, ready to defend ourselves but only for a brief moment because we cannot see alternatives, we do not feel whole and grounded. So, we mumble in defeat, blame, complain, and pass the gesture to the other to "hang in there."

When you, as a leader, can honour that this exists and is a gift of opportunity to rise, you will deliver exceptional results from the fullness of each and every person's limitless energies, starting with yours. When you honour this, you understand that others will learn, heal, grow, and achieve from their true source of limitless energies, when you are able to live it, model it, encourage it, because you foster it yourself. You will anoint yourself as a great leader that embodies leadership in all aspects of your life – you make a difference through your leadership that spans rewards, for and beyond the organizational world.

The FACTOR approach is an invitation to guide you in your transformative success journey. The pages preceding outlined the key aspects to this approach, what will guide you and what guides me as I guide others when I work with them. This book intends to serve my intention to impress upon you the credo that the FACTOR approach invites you to lead the way, in the name of Love.

Summary

Believe that achieving lasting success in anything starts and permeates from within and it takes habitual authentic self-awareness, potential for greatness, purpose, goals, and daily habits for balance in all aspects of life because they all matter simultaneously – relationships, personal, business/career, body/health, financial, recreation/leisure time, and contribution/legacy, within the context of love, connection, and joy.

Zero in on and tap into your unique possibilities for "extraordinary" and the inner power of thoughts and actions in the context of love, connection, and joy. Know that from this, we are able to tap into this "extraordinary" waiting to be unleashed for every aspect of our life – thereby raising the bar on personal and professional engagement, success growth, blending into leadership, enabling, and empowering ourselves to reach our goals/results and pay it forward to make a difference in all areas of our life, and in the lives of those around us.

Enable and inspire people to create meaningful success by deliberate design and engagement, in the context of love and joy.

Framing for Success Focus. Your mindset is the foundation for framing your focus to achieving successful results. Build this foundation on core fundamentals for success:

- Awareness;
- Taking full responsibility for your outcomes;
- Having a clarity of purpose;
- Having a clarity for what you want; and
- Create a frequency to attract what you want, not what you don't want.

Actions. Make them count. Take only those actions that stick to the success you want. Recognize the obvious actions and the inspired actions that serve your purpose. Make your actions stick to the success you want, by taking immediate action, planning, and setting goals, and taking immediate action to keep your momentum going.

Commit to Model Accountability. Hold to your agreements; don't make commitments you cannot keep; model accountability; enable others to act from their core genius; commit to continuous improvements.

Taking Care of Transforming for Success. Practice self-care by taking care of your transformation for success. Honour your past, present and future successes. Declutter your mind space, through declutter habits; transform your negative inner-coach to a positive inner-coach; surround yourself with like-minds and tribal supporters.

Out of the Comfort Zone. Be open to success clues within the trying times in your journey so that you can break through comfort zones that don't serve you; practice fearless grit; break through your barriers and get to your fabulous achievement line.

Relationships Matter. Know the relationships that matter to you and for your authentic success – build, strengthen and nurture them to sustain healthy relationships with self and others. From this, communities and organizations will ultimately benefit.

And just in case, you feel you need it…

Survival Guidelines for Your Transformation Journey

Guideline 1: Understand and live by acceptance. Accept your clarity and purpose and stop second-guessing yourself. Just do it.

Guideline 2: Don't judge. Don't assume. Ever. Focus on your process not product.

Guideline 3: Defend your cause and process. You'll inevitably run into someone who'll challenge your cause and process or will want you to do it only a certain way. Consider the source. Are they you? Do what you need to do.

Guideline 4: Never let anyone tell you what to create or how to be. Yes, be open to feedback, suggestions, guidelines. Create and act from your choice, grounded on your purpose and faith because you've already considered others in your creation.

Guideline 5: Be healthy in mind, soul, emotions, body, and commit to this – know what you have to do to, maintain this health and do it.

Guideline 6: Practice wholeness. This includes grieving when you need to, accepting the whole you, welcoming your losses, and gains, weaknesses and strengths, blah-moments, and awesome moments. We have an idea that success is a happy occasion. It can also be lonely, isolating, and disappointing. Give yourself the space to feel whatever you feel, and don't feel as though you shouldn't have a wide range of emotions. Emotions are emotions, and are natural part of us, not intended to be denied. Practice wholeness in every moment. Bring yourself back to your centre and give yourself an inner and outer big smile from ear to ear. Then model and foster this with others.

Guideline 7: Create your brilliant reality from the place of love. Wear it with pride and give the skeptics the "raspberry" or a smile (that smile from guideline 6). Create and express from your purpose, right at them.

Guideline 8: Remember that the part of you that creates brilliance is that inner highest self of yours. Allow your highest self to welcome to share the love and joy you get from your highest self and have tribe mates join in from their highest self. Take care of each other, hold each other accountable, spread the love and the magnificence.

Guideline 9: Listen to your favourite inspirational tunes (make sure Queen's "Under Pressure" is there. Ooh, and Michael Jackson's "Man in the Mirror"). And while you're at it, grab a few mirrors and make them your "believe-mirrors" – always make one within your reach – they make for your fool-proof cheering section.

Guideline 10: Don't pay attention to the odds. Trust yourself. There is no such things as "woo-woo" when it comes to love. Love is not a ludicrous topic to encourage in leadership; it's essential. Pray and accept help from others and whatever source in this world offers it, remembering that God is behind it all, waiting for our full expression of gratitude and thanks through our highest self.

Guideline 11: The "mother-of-all guidelines." Be grateful daily for your past, present, and future to come. Don't just practice it like it's another repetitive routine you can easily overlook in meaning. Feel every word of your gratefulness, be specific and feel it.

Love to lead the way, to live leadership, and to make a difference.

FURTHER READING

The Success Principles by Jack Canfield
The 7 Habits of Highly Effective People by Stephen R. Covey
Principle-Centred Leadership by Stephen R. Covey
Primary Greatness by Stephen R. Covey
Mega Living! 30 Days to a Perfect Life by Robin Sharma
The Science of Being Well by Wallace D. Wattles
The Science of Success: The Secret of Getting What You Want by Wallace
    D. Wattles
The Secret by Rhonda Byrne
Real Power by James A. Autry & Stephen Mitchell
The Seven Spiritual Laws of Success by Deepak Chopra
Mindset: The New Psychology of Success by Carol S. Dweck, Ph.D.
Oneness With All Life by Eckhart Tolle
The Road Less Travelled by Scott Peck

ACKNOWLEDGEMENTS

This book would not even have started, let alone completed, without the great love and support of several people in my life. They say behind every successful person is a special person supporting them. I truly am blessed because that "special person" is more, a tribe of fantastic human beings. To all of you, I owe my deepest gratitude. What follows is most certainly an incomplete list and does not do my thanks full justice without my ongoing time I promise to give and share with you in our lifetime together.

To my wide-eyed and sometimes teen-eyes-rolled, son, Joshua, who even at the age of seventeen, gets it that Mom is up to something she believes in. Thank you immensely for welcoming who I am and being in your life. Thank you for all you're teaching me and for giving me that extra special inspiration for why I do what I do in the name of love.

To my brothers, Joel, Moses, and Darren. Thank you, thank you, for making your one and only blood-sister feel and know that I'm always loved and supported. You have been my built-in best friends since birth.

To Mom and Dad, without your love and support over the years, all of the lessons I've learned from you, this book, my passion for contributing to a healthy humankind, and the work I do with others, might never have happened. Thank you for all you do and are to me.

To my circle of friends which span nation-wide, and around the world, truly. Without each of your special part in my life, I would not have even started my journey of setting dreams and aiming to achieve. I am truly blessed by the support and endless belief each of you have in me, in my dreams, and in my continual journey of expressing myself in the context of love and joy for all. Thank you for putting up with my incessant natters of work and ideas, for the memory-building laughter, tears, life insights and communal support shared to remind me of the vitalness of friendship. Special thanks to my "sister from another mother," Kari, for the decades of tried and true unwavering belief and support in the years of my self-discovery. For funding me generously throughout my entire writing journey, and through my darkest moments in the years, being a beacon because you believed in me when I could not. Special thanks to my dear niece, Danielle, for keeping me charged and in warm company during my writer's block. Special thanks to Michele, Michelle, Charlotte, Jenn, Rhonda, Karen and my "beavers" crew for each of your uniquely special ways in having kept me sane and social when I became excessively reclusive and doubted myself in my creative writing frenzy.

To my clients, thank you for your trust. I am honoured by you and I'm grateful that my work with you inspires me each day to shape my next messages and contributions for a healthy human kind. My special thanks also go to those who specifically inspired me to include nuggets in this book.

To my professional and personal transformation mentors: Jack Canfield and his Canfield team, my entrepreneurial business coach Colin Sprake through his Make Your Mark program and team; and my author coach and mentor, Angela Lauria and her team at The Author Incubator. Thank you for your support in my core genius, my skills-growth, and my ongoing personal transformation to enable my message to make a difference in my life and the lives of others.

In collaboration with the team at The Author Incubator I also acknowledge, with thanks and appreciation, the Morgan James Publishing Team: David Hancock, CEO & Founder; my Author Relations Manager, Gayle West; and special thanks to Jim Howard, Bethany Marshall, and Nickcole Watkins.

THANK YOU

I am so grateful for the opportunity you took me up on in reading my book. I hope it provided you with some great nuggets to help you in your leadership journey while also gaining momentum, and quick-hit tips on how you can start applying techniques immediately. There was a lot of high-level information I covered in this book, including my framework and approach with my clients. It would be my honour to provide you with deeper context on these tools – how they can fit into your transformation journey. If you're curious to learn more, and to keep your momentum going, contact me at maria.nebres@factorof.com.

Here are some of extras I would love to offer you as a thank you, along with ways I can further help you go through your strategies I discussed in the book:

1. Free Strategy Session: I'll include your answers to the questions and tips of trial actions I outlined in my book

2. Free introductory learning tools discussed in my book for you and your team

3. A video-intro overview of how I can help, featuring and endorsed

by Jack Canfield, author of *The Success Principles* and co-author of the *Chicken Soup for The Soul* book series

Here's to your success and making a difference through your leadership, in the context of love!

ABOUT THE AUTHOR

Maria Nebres is the founder of MPCS Inc. and The Factor Of Corporation which provides a unique blend of integrative services for achieving breakthrough results through her FACTOR method. With over 25 years of human resources and gained human relations insights to the development and realization of success potential, Maria has served her clients across diverse industries including healthcare, financial services,

Photo credit: Roger Smith, Make up by Roger Inc.

pharmaceutical, translation services, foodservice, technology, research and development, management consulting, and the public sector.

Her practice includes a service dedicated to providing authentic success guidance, applicable in all areas of personal achievement and business-related goals, after having found her groove from being inspired by motivated people, healthy relationships, leading experts and motivational speakers/teachers in the field of mindset transformation for success management. She was awarded her certification to teach The Success Principles from the Canfield Training Group, certified in psychometric assessment tools, and is an active member of the World Association of Female Professionals (AOFP).

Maria's F.A.C.T.O.R. framework follows a person-centred approach through six key iterative phases guiding her clients in their transformation work: 1) Framing a foundation for success, 2) actions to make success stick, 3) committing to success with accountability, 4) taking care of transformation, 5) orchestrating success by breaking through the comfort zone, and 6) relating for the heart of what matters for lasting results. Offering a time-tested universal framework for helping people to get unstuck in life's problem sources to success, she has been able to express her personal mission statement, "to enable and inspire people to create a fulfilling, authentic and successful life deliberately designed in a context of love and joy."

Her deliberate design of her own life and career has gained her a clear and focused path to success while helping others, despite the challenges she faced in her own life. Her success journey of personal transformation through abuse, toxic relationships and health struggles, have gracefully transformed her life and career from what she calls her "blessings in disguise." These blessings have ultimately inspired her to learn from her challenges and transform them into valuable skills and services that have created the "why" for her service to others. She continues to be inspired to share the values of a healthy mindset and relationships, passion, focus and drive for action-oriented solutions to achieve success. Today, she feels blessed by her large circle of loved ones near and far, and lives with her beautiful son, Josh, and their adorable pug-mix dog, Theo, in the greater north-end area of Toronto, Canada. Contact: maria.nebres@factorof.com

Printed in the USA
CPSIA information can be obtained
at www.ICGtesting.com
JSHW022332140824
68134JS00019B/1445